This Song Has No Title

Me and Her
A Tale of Two Ditties

JIM LUCITT

outskirtspress

DENVER, COLORADO

Outskirts Press, Inc.
http://www.outskirtspress.com

ISBN: 978-1-4787-7681-9

Outskirts Press and the "OP" logo are trademarks belonging to Outskirts Press, Inc.

PRINTED IN THE UNITED STATES OF AMERICA

For Stephen

Day 1-

Well, that was easy.

Truth be told, it always was easy. The only thing or person that ever made it hard for me was…me. I always had some excuse. I always had to follow some oddball ritual leading up to it. It had to be on a specific date or day of the week. I had to time it out so that my last cigarette in the pack was my last one for the night, and after I'd smoked it appreciatively but disgustedly, I'd toss all my smoky, foul-smelling clothing into the wash and floss and brush my teeth vigorously and rinse and then climb into bed, certain that the next day would be better. A fresh new start. I was always convinced that quitting smoking, each time, it was going to be for good. After all, for every time in my life that I had started to smoke, I had quit. I just made it so hard for myself. For all of my past procrastinating, fidgeting, and hand-wringing ignorance in trying to break a senseless routine and habit, this time, it just somehow happened differently.

It was April and a graduation was coming up for one of my daughters. It was the middle of the week, and I started my day like any other. Morning chores after a drop-off at school for the youngest one. A couple of cups of coffee, and, of course, a couple of Marlboros out in the backyard. I dressed for my mid-day shift and headed off to work and even got halfway through it when it just came over me. Without so much as a thought or a care, after smoking down a 'Boro on a break and feeling the usual overwhelming sickly feeling from it, I butt it out on the ground with my boot and then proceeded to empty out the remainder of the pack. I crushed them somewhat haphazardly, crumpled the box, and then, along with my lighter, tossed the whole mess in the trash and turned to go back to work.

When I got home that night, I still wreaked of tobacco, so no one noticed any real difference in the smelly old man that came through the door. I really wasn't paying much attention myself, and perhaps that's why it worked. No words or comments were necessary. It just was what it was.

Day 2-

I woke up that next morning in a world that was no different from the one I had fallen asleep in. I was still old, bent, and ugly, about 53, which I had turned about 2½ months ago. It was in April that my wife had just reached her 50th, and I'd thrown a huge party for her. Real huge. And I'd quit smoking just before my birthday, but it didn't last, and I used this big night as an excuse to break it gently to everyone that I'd already eased back into my obnoxious habit. It was the stress of planning this massive event. There was lots of money spent at the restaurant for catering and wine and drinks and, well, hell, I was gonna enjoy myself, and after the big surprise entrance, no one was gonna miss me while I disappeared out the back door...

I was still employed by the county as a wage earner, in a position I detested, and my future with them was as bleak as ever. On the bright side, the family had just moved in the first of March to a newer, larger house in a better neighborhood. We'd left behind our old home of 17 years.

But the brightest moment came to me that morning when I awakened fully to realize that I was still the father of two of the smartest, sweetest, most loving, happy, and, of course, beautiful, young ladies. Both July babies, born 2 years apart, the oldest would be 16 and starting to drive. The younger of the two was the soon-to-be graduate and soon-to-enter high school. They were not just the brightest light in my life, they were my whole world. Still are. And they were all my reasons for living. And it was time to wake up, take a deep breath, get up, start the new day, and see them both off to school.

Awhile back, Willie Nelson and Merle Haggard had recorded a song called, "Reasons to Quit." I'm not sure who, if either of them, actually penned it, but it was a catchy tune and it filled my head as I pulled on yesterday's clothes, which I was certain still wreaked of tobacco. The song wasn't just about smoking (and quitting), but hard living, and ultimately, trying to live with bad decisions by making better ones. The refrain went something like,

"and the reasons to quit…are getting bigger every day."

That was it in a nutshell, I thought, as I left my bedroom and headed down the stairs to see their sleepy, but smiling, faces in our kitchen. Again, I knew that it was useless to make any announcements or statements about what I had done the day before, and with the stale stench of smoke about me, I knew my cover wasn't going to be blown any time soon.

But there they were, sitting at the island counter, seemingly just for no other purpose but to light up my dismal, depressing life and spin my world around. My reasons to quit. Getting bigger every day.

Day 3-

I had weekends off, and the next one was coming up quick, and that was usually a time for anxiety and even apprehension whenever I was freshly into a "new quit." Let's face it, I started smoking when I was 9 and started drinking by age 13, and doing everything else a good ol' American boy does while he's coming of age, and cigarettes always went hand in hand with everything I did, every day. And now, weekends had come to represent a break from the grind, a time for relaxing and rewinding, although with drug testing at my job and having grown into the parenthood thing for a good spell now, a cocktail or two was the only acceptable vice or form of release, and weekends were the only acceptable time.

Usually, this was the time to fret. I simply could not have a beer or a glass of wine without an immediate craving—and need—for a cigarette. I had not had even a sip since my wife's birthday bash and really didn't miss it. So this time, with things just happening so differently, but easily, the thought of the coming days off just after my shift came to me lightly, and I embraced the lofty feeling. *Bring it,* I thought to myself.

Day 4-

Saturday morning arrived. I'd made it through Friday night without anyone else in the house any wiser to the change. The girls were all very socially active in those days and usually involved in some sort of evening outing that was followed by networking on their phones or computers. No one really noticed me coming in the night before, and no one really paid much attention when I awoke. This was nothing new, as with the different shift times that my wife and I worked, and the fact that I snored terribly and therefore had to have my own room to sleep in, it was rare that my movements ever solicited much attention. I had given up coffee the morning after my final cigarette. I had to. All caffeine. No one had noticed that either. So I headed for the fridge and looked inside for something to get me going. Something different. Something, maybe…healthy? I opted for some cereal and cold milk, and it was wonderful as I seemingly tasted and enjoyed every bite like I never had before. I got around to my chores, which were minimal and simple, but then, with the whole day ahead of me and nothing but time on my hands, I had to truly address my new lifestyle change for the first time.

The girls all clamored about throughout the house, but eventually they gathered together for some sort of errand running. Soon the house was empty and quiet. And now for the first time in over 3 days, I was beginning to get that uncomfortable feeling of nicotine withdrawals. The "Jones." But I knew just how to handle it.

I reached for my iPod.

"Music is the healing power."

I love music. A lot. All kinds. It is a very big part of my life, and who I am.

Years before, those words came to me in a song titled, "Beggar in Blue Jeans," sung by Peter Rowan and his brothers, Chris and Lorin. Since I was feeling much like the subject in the song at that moment, I thought turning to music was the best move for many reasons.

It may be an understatement to say that music is a big part of my life. Besides my girls, it was pretty much my whole world. Still is. And it is not only one of the biggest common denominators I have had with the people in my life, it has often been the glue that has held me fast to those folks.

My brother Stephen (hell, all my family), my wife, and all my friends, and now, my two girls. I shared it all with all of them and taught everyone all I knew about music, and now my girls were sharing theirs and teaching me.

And years after that song had been released, a dear friend of mine would share something that would help to heal me, with music, and change my life forever.

I met Scott through the parish church and school that my daughters attended, and our daughters and wives had all become close friends. We not only formed a rockin' little carpool for the girls, we forged a bond of friendship that has withstood to this day. Scott was a professional musician with a music recording and publishing company and, like the rest of his family, witty, whip smart, and kinda wild...a lot of fun to be around, and we'd all hang out as much as we could.

Our families also enjoyed the better things in life that were afforded by the Apple Computer Corporation. I was certainly the least tech savvy of this entire group, usually depending on my girls to guide me, but we all managed to get along and get through the modern world together with our Macintosh machinery. Then one day, while waiting to sign up for an annual family event at our church school that involved our families having to cue up for a good part of the afternoon outside the parish hall, while others read magazines or talked on cell phones, Scott nonchalantly pulled an iPod out of his pocket. I didn't quite grasp it at first. Call me slow. Even with a barrage of advertising and the heavy promotion of its arrival, I was, quite honestly, clueless as to what this device was, or what it was all about.

But I should have known that Scott would be the first to have one of these gadgets, and I have been ever grateful for that moment when I learned that he was.

It was old school. Not anything like the sleek numbers in today's market. It was bulky and fat, somewhere between a deck of cards and, yes, a pack of cigarettes, but it weighed about as much as a chunk of brick. I was fascinated from the moment he slipped on the tiny earbuds and started to sway with the joyful noise that only he could hear. So, being slow, but intrigued, I asked him about it as the others around us nodded in recognition of his new toy and the acceptance that he, naturally, was the first to sport one.

I was floored. My head began to spin. I was still not even aware of how to navigate the Mac at home to download music and create my own library.

I wasn't processing this too well, and then finally, he placed the slab in my palm and positioned the earbuds for me and pressed a button. "Sundown," by Gordon Lightfoot. And my head exploded. And the rest is a blur. But I do recall going home that night and grabbing whichever young female house-hold member was available between the kitchen and the bedrooms and the bathrooms and took instructions from each one, feverishly taking in each technological step to launch a collection of my own. I went on a binge. More like a terror. I smoked and drank my way through each spare minute of the entire 2 weeks that followed, using every electronic stereo option now at my fingertips to amass all the best and all of my favorite pieces of music from record, radio, and tape, to the wall of CDs in our home office, including mine, my wife's, and my children's, to create my very own music library. And when it was all over I was the King of the World. Yeah, it was only rock and roll...but I liked it.

It was late autumn, but that only meant that both the holidays and my birthday were looming up quickly. The one last factor in this huge new musical equation was about to be entered, and Santa Claus was real good to me that Christmas. Like a kid in a candy store, I eagerly and breathlessly tore open this most anticipated gift. Another brief binge ensued, but it lasted only as long as it took to sync up my grand new present to the computer, when I was then cleared for takeoff and wheels up. There had never been a sweeter sound than that hum of the Macintosh and no greater, fulfilling sight than to watch all the elements wink, flash, and buzz before my eyes until the tech task was complete. Just like the days of my youth when I would tuck my transistor radio beneath my pillow at night and let myself be serenaded to sleep by the AM sounds, I think I may have had those earbuds planted in my skull for most of that holiday season. And better yet, I knew I would soon be going to visit my younger brother, Stephen, and I could rattle his social, musical cage just like mine had been.

Like me, Stephen loved music. We both grew up with our dad's collection of 78 rpm records of everything from Hoagy Carmichael to John Philip Sousa to the classical symphonies. We both endured our oldest brother's tastes for Frank Sinatra and Jack Jones, on to the next brother's more eclectic flavorings of dance, soul, rock, and blues on the 33 rpms.

The next brother brought us all together in the house with the Beatles and the Rolling Stones and endless 45 rpm singles. I went on to raise my little brother with the Grateful Dead, Waylon Jennings, and John Hiatt. Stephen would repay me by schooling me with the likes of everyone from U2, the Neville Brothers, The Clash, and Sonia Dada to Carlos Santana, Bonnie Raitt, Robert Cray, and Prince. And when we finally got together and I presented my newly minted iPod for the first time, he gazed upon it much like I did, as if it were the Holy Grail. As if it were handed down directly to us, from God himself. From that moment on, we both knew that, together, the two of us would enter into the Great iPod Merger Cluster Consortium, melding the most magnificent assortment of musical magic in "our" world, in "our" lifetime. It would not be long until Stephen had his own iPod, and the race was on, the two of us hustling, plotting, scheming, creating, and trading, but mostly, sharing.

Life was always good when Stephen and I were together, and even better because of the music that always played in our world...our own little soundtrack. Life was good. The world was magic. The music was glue.

Oftentimes though, looking back, I'd wonder if r real glue was Stephen himself. You see, he was younger tnan I, but he was bigger and wiser, brighter and bolder. I was the steady ship that sailed a set course—a decent job, wife, and kids, in a nice home. He was the pirate vessel tossing about with sails torn. Single, wild, handsome, and very outgoing. While we both oftentimes felt that we were living our lives vicariously through the other, we both always respected that we were our own men, navigating from different charts, across the vast oceans of life.

But what was also understood but never said was there could always be another me, but there could never be another Stephen, and we were both OK with that.

So it was, that these thoughts and many others filled my head that Saturday afternoon and on into that evening as I kept myself busy and quite happily away from cigarettes, all the while with my earphones secured to each side of my head while my iPod flowed forth with the powerful music that would heal me.

Day 5-

"Sunday Morning Comin' Down," by Kris Kristofferson, was, oddly enough, the song that was waiting for me on the iPod the next morning when I came to. It seemed from the start that this was going to be my hardest day yet, and I became a bit anxious as I stirred about in my bed, but eventually I rolled out of it and faced the music.

I had to get innovative and thought that I had when I remembered the last time that I had quit, while living at the old house, and still fairly new to this iPod concept. I had taken to walking each day, usually after the morning carpool and before my matinee shift at work. It seemed to work for quite a while, but after a few rough months, I fell back into the smoke and would find myself hustling through my walk with my music just so I could get home quickly, strip off my clothes, and choke down a couple of cigarettes before and after I ate, and then shower away the stench and convince myself that I could live a lie the rest of the day until the next. A lie to myself.

Still, this time was going to be different, and that was all the convincing I needed. I pulled on my shorts and a T-shirt and laced up my raggedy old sneakers and plugged in ol' Kris and bounded down the stairs and out the door. I thought that the three ladies of the house might have been there in the kitchen, but I had the music turned all the way up and really didn't want to stop to chat or answer any questions, and therefore, never really noticed if they were or not.

I was a tad stiff, to say the least, and out of shape like nobody's business. I stopped at the wall at the end of the walkway and attempted some rather juvenile stretching exercises and threw in a couple of jumping jacks. That was quite enough, and off I strode, suddenly realizing that, unlike the old neighborhood, I had no idea where I was headed. However, I did know that there was a huge expanse of land just a few blocks away that held not just a park, but two golf courses, along with tennis and basketball courts and three or more baseball diamonds, and even (I would soon discover) an archery range.

After Kris was done, I'd gone just a couple of blocks, already feeling tired and winded. Letting the music flow through the "shuffle" mode helped to keep me focused though as I eagerly anticipated what little surprises might be next. In fact, I rarely ever chose a genre or artist and I had not yet mastered the art of compiling personal playlists, so the unknown would always seem to work best. "All Down The Line" by the Rolling Stones. It was prefect! And now it was coming back to me…while folk music or flamenco guitar or even the Mormon Tabernacle Choir might have seemed quaint or even apropos for a Sunday morning stroll, it was always going to be the upbeat, hard-core rock that would set me to moving a little more quickly, taking some of that heavy load off my tired, old feet. Mick Jagger and the classic, pounding bite of Keith Richards's guitar had never failed me before.

I was now out on the big boulevard just across from the first golf course, and it offered huge, shady trees along its side that seemed to draw me into the crosswalk toward them, so off I went…all down the line, indeed.

There was just enough sloping and rising in the sidewalk to work my leg muscles a bit, and I worked on my breathing technique as well. I was so much more aware of the elements and my surroundings and the sights and sounds that the world was offering. "People Got To Be Free" by The Rascals popped up on the pod and the soundtrack to the moment was undeniably perfect, and…*"all the world over, it's so easy to see, people everywhere just want to be free"* played as I passed the other humans along the way. Young and old, from all walks of life, all seemingly out for the same reason. Being free and enjoying life and trying to be healthy, and damn…just like me!

Sure, I realized, I don't get around much anymore, and when it comes to being hip, I'm slower than paychecks…but I'll be damned if nearly every single one of them had an iPod as well! And now that was the first thing I was noticing about the folks around me. Walking, running, off to play golf or tennis, everyone seemed to have some sort of earphones or headset and some sort of audio device attached to them. For the most part, they looked to be quite happy, and I was starting to feel the same as the Beatles came into my head next with "I Feel Fine." Yeah, *"she's in love with me and I feel fine,"* they sang and I thought of my wife as I watched a young gal approach me in a jog and then looked past her to see another young lady not far behind, both with earphones. *I'm gonna like this,* I thought to myself as I nodded and smiled at each one of them in passing.

I managed to work my way around the park real estate and found my way home, discovering a few rather steep hills along the way and decided that this was going to be the perfect work-out for me. I am nothing if not a man of routines and rituals, and I was certain that this walk would become a daily outing. It took me just about an hour, looking in at the clocks in the small shops that lined the big avenue that I had now returned to, and I was becoming curious if I had covered any substantial ground. Upon my return home, I bounded up the steps, boldly blowing through the front door, and there they were…my reasons to quit. The oldest, almost gleefully, blurted out, "Daddy, did you quit smoking?!?!" She was usually the first to notice, and probably the one that most wanted me to quit each time I did, and it was always her that seemed to be most disappointed in me every time I fell back into it. I didn't have an answer for her; it was too soon, but the genuine sparkle in her eyes drew a return sparkle from my own, and I just nodded my head in hopes for her approval on any level.

With that, I grabbed the keys to my motorcycle. It was a fairly new Harley that never got enough attention, but now was the time to show it some. I fired it up and let it run just enough to get the "juices flowin'," zeroed out the odometer, and took off back around the path that I'd just done on foot.

From my driveway and back it was exactly 3.1 miles, 5K. Perfect. *I am so going to do this again,* I thought. Every day.

Day 6-

Monday morning meant back to the humdrum of work and school starting with the carpool, but I had woken up feeling rather energized and excited. The trip with the young one went quickly, and I found myself racing home for my jaunt with my music. The weather was perfect, and I was feeling pretty darn good about my decisions this time around. Everything seemed to be falling into place neatly. By the time I reached the big boulevard, I began to notice things again. Traffic was heavier, and there was definitely more engine exhaust all about, and the number of folks out for healthy recreation was significantly lower. I took notice of the folks I passed by and was again keenly aware of their headsets.

Day 7-

My having quit smoking was wonderfully far from my thoughts. Work was just there, and I was sleeping well, but, man, I was just living through it all to get out for my morning stroll.

On only my second weekday out, I was now spotting the regulars. There was the slightly older lady that reminded me of a first-grade teacher. Another older gal walked in long pants. Lots of people walking and running their dogs; couples and parents, jogging with strollers, all of them with earbuds and audio. Definitely, fewer young women than the weekend, but I guess that would be a typical observation from an old hack of a dude like me. I was blessed to have the woman that I was married to that loved me as I loved her, but I wasn't dead yet. If the ones passing by could find it in them to nod or say good morning, it was great. If not, that was cool too.

But I had found that when a happy, healthy woman came

by, whether she would acknowledge me or not, it brought a smile to my soul and maybe even a grin to my face. And that was because, no matter the person or profile, it was a sense of like-mindedness that was bringing me happiness because, with each of them there was the audio...

Whereas I could be listening to anything from heavy metal to Beethoven, I couldn't help but wonder obsessively what they might be listening to. I had cleared the steepest part of my new daily journey. That came about 2 miles in and was approaching the turn that would send me downhill all the way home. Far up the street, I spied a young lady with a big dog as they crossed the road and ran off down an adjacent street. The only thing I noticed from that far back was that she too had an iPod, but I really wasn't thinking about all that anymore as John Hiatt filled my head with "Stood Up," as he lamented about a woman he'd left behind, one with flaming red hair.

Day 8-

Feeling great. Life was good. Happy to be alive and breathing and seeing the regulars. The first-grade teacher. The woman in long pants. A new face looking harassed by the baby in the stroller she was pushing. A nice old couple that talked to each other as they walked and didn't have any headphones on. I was on the first long stretch along the boulevard and shaded by the trees as I looked ahead and caught my first glimpse of her. I think it actually may have been the dog that I spied first, but I recognized them both immediately as the duo that had passed before me toward the end of the previous day's walk. And again, it was the dog that I seemed to fixate on as they approached, but that changed quickly as I locked my gaze upon the young

woman at the other end of the leash, seemingly tryin
to keep up with the large Labrador retriever. No so
sense the presence of her iPod then it all ended. No, she hadn't
quite finished passing me by, but it ended. My life. I think. Or
thought. At that moment, that seemed frozen now in time...

And then it did end. She and the dog both trotted on past
and were gone. Of course, I turned my head and tried to soak
in every detail about this lady that had just caused my heart to
skip, race, and sink—all at once. No, it was not just because I'm
a dude and that's what most dudes do. It was a movement that
was completely beyond my control. It was, plain and simply, a
phenomenon self-control would not regulate. As my heart re-
gained its regular beat and my pulse had recovered, I realized
that my mouth was agape, and that I had slowed in my steps.
Slowed, perhaps, because my legs and feet had become unre-
sponsive and were not registering quite right with the neurons
and synapses upstairs, and therefore, one was not following the
other. But don't get me wrong. I love my wife. Still do. Always
will. Put no one before her. Ever. And, she's hot. Still is. But I
didn't really take in what the woman jogger looked like, except
for one minor thing. It was a blur. A flash. A physically and
mentally crashing moment that I will never get back. A cosmic,
passing vortex that grabbed me and shook me, and then tossed
me thunderously aside, like some cheap special effect in a bad
sci-fi flick. I mean, I was just out walking and listening to music. I wasn't looking for this kind of shit to happen. I then immediately felt stupid, like a little kid. A school yard kid that got
caught with his eyes wildly ablaze over the new redheaded girl
on the playground.

That's it! That's what I got! The red hair.

OK, now, I know all about that old stereotype when it comes
to redheads. It's not what made the whole moment so damned

weird. It was just all that this walking wounded boy could salvage from the debris of what had just happened. "She Was Hot," by the Rolling Stones, began to penetrate my psyche by way of the shuffle mode on my iPod. Indeed. Thought I was, *"goin' off the rails, ridin' down a pleasure trail."*

Then it occurred to me that my steps had properly resumed, one foot in front of the other, and I was now more keenly aware of Jagger's lyrics and Keith and Ronnie's staccato guitar dueling. So on I went, none the wiser or any more pleased with what I had taken from that freakish bomb blast, but that hot red hair.

Day 9-

Work was rough the night before. And my sleep was even worse. Make no mistake, I was what I can only describe as shaken. Confused? Yeah, that too. Dumbfounded. Consumed. I even checked the local newspaper for the lunar forecast. But once the carpool duties were done with this morning, I was laced up and briskly walking back out to the parkland and even looking forward to whatever may come next. And come it did. First, a straggle of the regulars. Then a glance at my watch, to give myself a time reference.

Then I noticed my pace, which had quickened a bit, and my focus, which was now far and straight-ahead of me. "Have You Seen Her Face" by The Byrds opened up in my ears. I had not yet, but I could sense it coming, and I fell back into a confused state over what had happened the day before while I thought about how best to describe it. This brought my forward movement down a notch, and my eyes dropped slightly too as my mind began to wander. Suddenly, I was feeling it again, and it hit me hard! Nitrous oxide! Yeah, that was it! Damn laughing gas! And not like the dentist's office...I'm talking about big, huge balloons full at Grateful Dead concerts or like you could find on Bourbon Street during Mardi Gras. If you've experienced it, you know full well what I'm talking about, and I was beginning to feel it again when I looked up to see why...It was her and she was running toward me with that big dog and I was going back into that nitrous meltdown and feeling giddy yet uncontrolled and elated but sort of comatose as well. She passed right by me as I tried desperately to catch new details about her when all I could really achieve was a glance, away from hers, as I attempted a weak smile and nod in her general direction. Jeez, could I have been any more boyish, juvenile, and just plain foolish? *Most likely not,* I thought as my "coming-down-from-laughing-gas" act subsided, and I trudged on, having gained nothing but gloom and despair, and I had not even turned to watch her pass me...

Day 10-

Friday. My workweek would be over later that evening, the carpool was complete, and I was on my way with my music and my striding. I was most concerned about seeing the redhead but not falling victim to the narcotic state that she would likely throw me into. Somewhere into my outing, about the last third of it, she had begun to approach me, towed by her oversized canine. I held up pretty well and got quite an eyeful as well as a mind full. She neared me like a television advertisement that I remembered from my childhood..."the closer she gets, the better she looks." Was it bath soap or skin cream, or whatever they were pushing in that ad, I don't know, but I did know that that old-timey vision of the beautiful woman in a summer dress dancing in slow motion toward her handsome man, longingly, waltzing in slow motion toward her in a field of fragrant flowers was happening in real time right now, right here on the street, and me and her were in that cheesy commercial.

And just like that TV commercial, the closer she got, good Lord, the better she looked! What I noticed first, from just slightly afar, was her run. More gallop than trot, had she been a horse; more panicked run than a simple jog for a young lady. The Labrador seemed to be in control and not being too forgiving of her not keeping up. Before I realized that, Dionne Warwick's "Walk On By" was breezing between my ears. She had passed but not without a most notable sequence—a very genuine smile and deep, dark eyes—the smile which said she was acknowledging me and most likely my obviously dorky, dumbfounded face, and then those eyes that said, "Don't you dare take this any further or bother me while I'm running." Fair enough, I conjured as she strode on by and The Tubes came over the wires with, "She's A Beauty." Yup. One in a million girls. Why would I lie? She's a beauty. And that was all I got, feeling only a slight trace of the narco-gas exhaust bombs I had felt on the days before.

Day 11-

The weekend had arrived, and I was feeling great, and it was mostly because everyone at my house seemed to be content to let me do my thing, alone, and were actually quite happy for me. All the girls took joy in seeing Dad up and out first thing in the morning, doing something better than firing up a smoke and gulping coffee and swallowing donuts. Without the routine of the carpool, I managed to get out a bit earlier than the days before and was off to a great start until I had just cleared my neighborhood and approached the big boulevard.

There she was. Red hair under a ball cap, iPod wires up in her ears, and lopping hopelessly behind the big dog. In another direction. I was only momentarily let down as I glanced into the nearest business for the clock to make note of the time, and then I made note of the song I was hearing in my head, Waylon Jennings's version of, "See You Around (On Your Way Down)."

But I continued on nonetheless and was trying to enjoy the sights and the sounds and the smells, all of which seemed to be keener without the haze and stench of tobacco whacking at my senses. I assessed my feelings as far as the abrupt sighting of the Redhead without really coming to any hard conclusion about them. I was happy to be in my own little world with my own music and thoughts, yet my mind would wander back to the girl, the hair, the dog, and her headphones as I was led into The Band playing, "Up On Cripple Creek." As my very clear head began to fog up just slightly with the thought of how my wife never really liked that song and I was only partial toward it myself, and just what didn't she like about it and what did I think that young girl might think of it, she came into view on what I guessed was her second trip, and The Band broke into the line that went something like, *"me and my mate were back at the shack, and we had Spike Jones on the box..."*

And that was it. She was approaching fast, at the mercy of the big dog, and this wasn't going to be any sort of moment for me to discover any more details or fine points about her and, well, what happened next was simple fate. With the dog about 20 feet in front of me, I pointed first at my earpods and then to hers, and casually threw out, "What's on the box?" Her eyes locked into mine as we lined up face-to-face in passing, and I nervously began to wonder if she even heard me, as I felt slightly relieved that I hadn't asked what she had "in" her "box," and then started to get that silly little boy feeling all over again, as she offered back in a very bewildered manner just over her shoulder toward me, "...wait, what?...um, oh...oh! The Clash!' Should I Stay Or Should I Go?'" And she turned her head back around and trailed off down the road as my ears and head filled with Joan Baez and, "A Satisfied Mind," and I thought to myself so many different thoughts. My God, that went well. Better than I could have asked for. She didn't get too perturbed with me as she never really did slow down or have to stop, and not like that dog was even gonna let her. What a good sport. And then, what a great song! And though it took a few seconds for the coin to drop and for me to get a dial tone, I realized, how apropos it was. And by the time Joan was done, I realized, how apropos for me as well. Next up I was treated to Israel Kamakawiwo'ole as he crooned away on his medley of "Somewhere Over The Rainbow/What A Wonderful World." And at that very moment, it was a wonderful world for me. Something so simple, so innocent, just fun, just playful, this passing interaction between two strangers had brought to me such great pleasure and a satisfied mind. I learned as a kid that "curiosity killed the cat," but "satisfaction brought him back." For that very short time that morning I had a satisfied mind and a happy heart and felt that I'd gone somewhere over the rainbow...

Day 12-

Sunday morning and it was just me and my music again, and I was happy, perhaps still in a glow from the morning before. I got out at just about the same time and made my way out to the boulevard and took in all the sights and started spotting the regulars and the not-so-regulars. Just as I hit the side of the golf course, I took in a wonderfully attractive young lady that seemed to be just gliding toward me, almost hydroplaning on a sheet of thin air, waving her arms back and forth and along her sides with her head held proudly, almost defiantly, high, in a manner that conveyed confidence and elegance. Brunette. Smooth, glossy, porcelain skin. I had to assume she was French. She just looked French. As she passed, everything changed as I nodded in her direction and smiled, and she dropped her eyes away from mine. She seemed a tad embarrassed, as did I, because I don't know much French beyond "bonjour" and "merci," and I couldn't even come up with a hello in English. I let it go, but from that moment on, I would always think of her as "Frenchie."

And after Frenchie was gone, I was on the lookout for the Redhead. Remember, I am a dude, and, yes, there was some sort of minimal physical attraction for this gal, but truly, all I wanted was to see if my little game would catch on or just die mercilessly. Again, I was certain that she, like most of the walkers and runners with headsets, did not want anything to do with obnoxious old farts like me, and especially did not want anyone or anything, slowing them down—or worse, breaking their stride or stopping them. I was also pretty certain that she just did not want to "play." So when she eventually came into sight that morning and proceeded to light up my world, I felt some trepidation but managed to hold my own as she came nearer. Immediately, I'd forgotten the game. I'd forgotten all things musical. For now, I was finally able to focus, as I never could before. As if for my benefit it seemed that time stood still as I cast my gaze upon her from head to toe and back again and noticed for the first time the perfection of everything about her. Her skin. And the freckles. Those stunning deep, dark, brown eyes.

That hair. And then I, Lord knows why, I found myself locking my look toward her left hand for a wedding band when I heard her voice and brought my eyes up to meet hers as she passed and quickly, excitedly, and very breathlessly barked out, "Tom Petty and The Heartbreakers, from Southern Accents, 'Don't Come Around Here No More!!'"

Holy shit!! I just got all kinds of stupid right then. I hadn't even coolly gestured with my finger to my earpiece as I was too busy being a dude in a perp walk trance and ogling her natural beauty when I got slapped good with more than I could have ever dreamed of, and she was almost gone down the road before I could recover with an equally breathless, "Good Morning, Little School Girl," by the Grateful Dead, from their first album!! Damn!! That was so cool, I thought to myself. Damn! I was thinking I might be on to something good here. It just seemed right. It seemed fun. I was happy, and I picked up my stride as I headed toward home, trying to remember each little detail in that sequence. Like the fact that she was more on top of the game than I was, and how she seemed to be a willing and eager player, while I, once again, looked like a foolish little schoolboy, like some kind of Charlie Brown around the Little Red-Haired Girl. But a schoolboy I was. Always learning. And happy now with my newfound knowledge.

Day 13-

Monday, with my carpool duty done and I'm out on the trek on time, for the weekday. I was anxious, yes. I was also oblivious to my actions, feelings, or emotions, or any potential consequences thereof. It really never occurred to me that I was doing anything but just what I wanted to do, as it was healthy, it made me happy, and hey, what could happen? So I was a little pleased as The Redhead came into sight that morning and I felt myself breaking out with a grin as she approached with her Labrador, and before I could get out something like, "keep it clipped," or "just a title," as I pointed at my ears with one hand and hers with the other, she offered up, "STYX!" and I countered with, "STONES!" And she was gone, and I was content and still grinning and pleased with myself when she appeared again on her second go-round and gave out a, "RATT!" to which I had only, "POISON!"

Day 14-

Her- "THE CARS!"
Me- "MIKE AND THE MECHANICS!" And on the next "round,
Her- "BIG AUDIO DYNAMITE!"
Me- "THE BLASTERS!"

Day 15-

Her- "LIVE!"
Me- "DEAD!" Till she came back again with,
Her- "PRINCE!"
Me- "QUEEN!"

Now, I was taken by her range of choices, and that was what I noticed, so maybe I was asking too much by still feeling a wanting for something more in this game. Don't get me wrong, and I certainly hoped that she would not either, but I felt like this could really go somewhere different, in perhaps some eclectic way. I had engaged her and she was kind in her participation with me, but something inside of me was longing for more, on what I would think to be, an intellectual level?

Day 16-

It was now Thursday, late into my walk, and I had not seen her as I began the stretch toward home with the Left Banke in my head singing, "Walk Away Renée," and when they came to the line about the *"empty sidewalks on my block are not the same"*…She came out of nowhere and was headed for me with the dog pulling her along. As usual, I began to get stupid at the sight of her but held up well enough to quickly realize that I had no idea or game plan of how to diplomatically ask for just a song's title, as I thought this might factor a little ease into this daily passing of our two minds and playlists, when she made it real easy on me instead, and with a warm and cheery smile, pointed up at her ears while I offered,

Me- GONE TO DENVER (Waylon Jennings)
Her- COLORADO (The Flying Burrito Brothers)

Phew! That was good. That was easy, I thought. But then I got what I should have been at least slightly accustomed to by now and that was her quirky way of slapping me upside the head from somewhere out in left field when she turned as she jogged on by and said to me over her shoulder in a bit of a cocky tone, "What's this for anyway?"

Wow. Shit, darling, I really hadn't gotten that far with all this just yet…but I turned over my shoulder as well and offered the first thing that popped into my head, and would actually come to be quite proud of it, when I tossed back my one-word response, "research." By then, I'd hit the signal to cross the big boulevard back to my neck of the woods and enjoyed an old classic by the Rolling Stones, "Under Assistant West Coast Promotion Man." Yes. I'm really, really sharp. Sure do earn my pay.

Day 17-

Friday and the carpool is done and I'm in a bit of a mood. Not necessarily a good one, just a mood. Can't put my finger on what is wrong or different in my world, but I seem to be sensing that a lot of it has to do with this walking thing. This getting healthy thing. This irregular routine. The girl, the music, the thoughts that have been running through my head. As I am walking along this wonderful morning, my brain is in a scramble and I'm likely overthinking every little thought...like, where is she? Is she avoiding me? Had I pissed her off, maybe crossed some line with her? What could it be? Then I began to think through the previous day; her question, and my response...Hey, it was innocent enough on her part to ask that, and truly clever on my part to have delivered that comeback so quickly. Or so I was thinking. Yeah. Research. That's right. But...research for what?! I mean, I thought I knew. But now I was in a quandary of my own creation.

Damn it! Yes. Research. About her. I suppose. Yes, I wanted to find out, to learn, to know, everything I possibly could about this exotic, mysterious, and shining bright young woman. But what for?!? Who cares?!? I mean, I love my wife, but I'm enjoying a bit of harmless fun. Am I taking it just a tad too far because I'm a little curious, maybe even slightly fascinated? And what about the simplicity that brought this all about? The music?

And there it was, I conceded. It was the music. Nothing more, nothing less.

It was then that I let go of my frenzied thought enough to comprehend the very music that was in my head just then— "Easy Wind," by the Grateful Dead, talkin' of how the wind was *"blowin' cross the bayou today,"* while I was letting my feelings blow off and away in much the same manner. When they got to the line about *"a whole lot of women out on the streets today,"* I looked far up the street to see the Redhead coming out from a side street. That left me to assume she was on her second go-round and that I'd probably not get in any further research on this particular morning...

Day 18-

The weekend was upon us, and I'd been able to get out a little earlier than normal. My head seemed uncluttered, and it was almost uncanny that I would spot the Redhead early on in my walk, and her run, as I also noted that she was alone, the first time I'd ever seen her without her Labrador.

Me- HELLO, I LOVE YOU (The Doors)
Her- GOODBYE STRANGER (Supertramp), and comin' back around...
Me- HELLO, GOODBYE (The Beatles)
Her- GOODBYE IS ALL WE'VE GOT LEFT TO SAY (Steve Earle)

Day 19-

Me- WHAT'S YOUR NAME? (Lynyrd Skynyrd)
Her- THEY CALL ME THE BREEZE (Lynyrd Skynyrd), and when she came back-
Me- HEY HEY GOOD LOOKIN' (Hank Williams)
Her- THAT'S NOT MY NAME (The Mavericks)

Day 20-

Me- GOT TO GET YOU INTO MY LIFE (The Beatles)
Her- GOTTA GET AWAY (The Rolling Stones), and then...
Me- WHAT DOES IT TAKE? (Junior Walker and the All-Stars)
Her- IT'S GONNA TAKE A MIRACLE (Deniece Williams)

Day 21-

Me- A SONG FOR YOU (Leon Russell)
Her- SING YOUR OWN SONG (Buddy Holly + Mickey Gilley), then...
Me- THE SINGER NOT THE SONG (The Rolling Stones)
Her- JUST A SONG (Dave Mason)

Day 22-

Me- IF YOU MUST GO (Brian Elmquist)
Her- GO NOW (The Moody Blues)...second trip
Me- WHEN IT GOES IT'S GONE, GIRL (Tompall Glaser)
Her- LET ME GO (The Rolling Stones)

Day 23-

Me- LET IT BE ME (The Everly Brothers)
Her- SEE YOU LATER, I'M GONE (The Marshall Tucker Band)...
    then
Me- YOU REALLY HAD ME GOING (Holly Dunn)
He- GOING, GOING, GONE (Marty Stuart)

Day24-

Me- WHO WROTE THE BOOK OF LOVE? (The Monotones)
Her- IT WASN'T ME (George Thorogood)

Day 25-

Me- CUTS LIKE A KNIFE (Bryan Adams)
Her- FIRST CUT IS THE DEEPEST (Rod Stewart)...and
Me- TOO MUCH BLOOD (The Rolling Stones)
Her- LET IT BLEED (The Rolling Stones)

Day 26-

Me- SINCE I FELL FOR YOU (Guns N' Roses)
Her- FREE FALLIN' (Tom Petty And The Heartbreakers)...then
    this
Me- FALLING FOR YOU (Lady Antebellum)
Her- DOWN IN THE HOLE (The Rolling Stones)

Day 27-

Me- I'VE ALWAYS BEEN CRAZY (Waylon Jennings)
Her- YOU MAKE ME CRAZY (Gnarls Barkley)…second time
Me- YOU'RE DRIVING ME CRAZY (Joe Turner)
Her- I'D HAVE TO BE CRAZY (Willie Nelson)

Day 28-

Me- DRIVE MY CAR (The Beatles)
Her- SHE RUNS HOT (Little Village) comin' back around…
Me- FLY ME TO THE MOON (Frank Sinatra)
Her- IF I HAD A ROCKET LAUNCHER (Bruce Cockburn)

Day 29-

Me- THE HIGHWAY IS MY HOME (Joe Ely)
Her- TAKE THE HIGHWAY (The Marshall Tucker Band) followed
    by…
Me- WHERE DO WE GO FROM HERE? (Waylon Jennings)
Her- PLEASE GO HOME (The Rolling Stones)

Day 30-

Me- IF NOT FOR YOU (George Harrison)
Her- WHY ME? (Kris Kristofferson) plus…
Me- TELL ME WHY (The Beatles)
Her- DON'T ASK ME WHY (Donna Jean Godchaux Band)

Day 31-

Me- IT TAKES A LOT TO LAUGH, IT TAKES A TRAIN TO CRY
   (Bob Dylan)
Her- SLOW TRAIN COMIN' (The Grateful Dead and Bob Dylan)
   with...
Me- IF THAT TRAIN RUNS ON TIME (Jake Richmond)
Her- BEAT IT ON DOWN THE LINE (The Grateful Dead)

Day 32-

Me- WAITING ON A TRAIN (Boz Scaggs)
Her- TRAIN IN VAIN (The Clash) and back around came this...
Me- RUNAWAY TRAIN (Tom Petty And The Heartbreakers)
Her- SMOKE ALONG THE TRACK (Dwight Yoakam)

Day 33-

Me- ALL MY EX's LIVE IN TEXAS (George Strait)
Her- PUT ME ON A TRAIN BACK TO TEXAS (Waylon Jennings)

Day 34-

Me- HAVE YOU EVER SEEN THE RAIN (John Fogerty)
Her- A HARD RAIN'S GONNA FALL (Leon Russell) followed
   by...
Me- RAININ' IN MY HEART (Neil Young)
Her- BABY, THE RAIN MUST FALL (Glenn Yarbrough)

Day 35-

Me- HERE COMES THE RAIN (The Mavericks)
Her- LET IT RAIN (Eric Clapton) with this…
Me- HOW MUCH RAIN (CAN ONE MAN STAND?) (George Jones)
Her- I'M ONLY HAPPY WHEN IT RAINS (Garbage)

Day 36-

Me- DRUNKEN POET'S DREAM (Ray Wylie Hubbard)
Her- ONE BOURBON, ONE SCOTCH, ONE BEER (John Lee Hooker) and…
Me- SCOTCH AND SODA (The Kingston Trio)
Her- GIN AND JUICE (Snoop Dogg)

Day 37-

Me- I'M GONNA DRINK CANADA DRY (David Allan Coe)
Her- IT'S MARTINI TIME (Reverend Horton Heat) plus…
Me- TONIGHT THE BOTTLE LET ME DOWN (Waylon Jennings)
Her- TONIGHT THE HEARTACHE'S ON ME (The Dixie Chicks)

Day 38-

Me- CIGARETTES AND WINE (Jason Isbell)
Her- RED, RED WINE (Neil Diamond) and then…
Me- CIGARETTES AND ALCOHOL (Rod Stewart)
Her- ALCOHOL AND PILLS (Todd Snider)

Day 39-

Me- THE CHOKIN' KIND (Waylon Jennings)
Her- CHUG-A-LUG (Roger Miller)

Day 40-

Wow. How cool was my world...I was thinking on my 40th day without a smoke...I'd quit a nagging and nasty, dirty habit and done so for good this time...I was thinking...and I'd gotten back into a good healthy habit with my daily excursions. It was a routine that I truly looked forward to, and I felt I was making it fun, not just for me, but also for a wonderful stranger that seemed very willing to play along. I mean, man, I was getting everything I could have wanted. I always said you could tell so much about a person by their record collection, and that was one of my big meters for measuring up a young lady on a first date or first visit to her place. And here was this Redhead with tastes in music and artists that not only mirrored my own, but in some instances, eclipsed them. Right?!? So, whatever "research" this may have appeared to be, for myself or her, I was certainly feeling like I was getting to know this stranger in the best possible way...by exchanging, right in the moment, random tidbits from our chosen musical worlds.

With all that thinking, though, after lacing up my walking shoes and striding outside that morning, music seemed to be the very thing that left my thoughts. In fact, I wasn't sure I had even pressed *Play* on my iPod to bring any music whatsoever into my mind as I hit the big street and almost immediately spied the Redhead coming toward me at a pretty good clip— and no dog...

Me: "Hey, I'm 40 days without a cigarette!"

Her: "Oh my God! That's so great!" she returned, with only a slight break in her pace, but one that I noticed rather painfully and regrettably as she then turned and continued past.

I felt like I had committed a sin by taking her out of sync, interrupting the Zen of her movement. But it was a very honest and positive response I told myself as my inner Charlie Brown started to come out and I was becoming convinced that I'd just blown this really good thing that I was so pleased with when I first awoke.

Day 41-

I had a rough night of sleep and wasn't really all together when I set out this particular morning. It didn't help as I trudged along and came ever closer to the end of my walk that I was realizing I had not seen the Redhead and that my good thing was likely at an end. Fortune seemed to present itself, though, as she came into sight and came closer to me, this time with her dog hauling her along. So what do I do but toss that good fortune right into the breeze as I stopped and raised my hands up, motioning for her to stop.

She looked perturbed at best but reluctantly came to a halt in front of me, and I went into my unrehearsed babble. I introduced myself quickly, but she was silent and offered no name in return as I explained, again, that I was newly in recovery from my tobacco use and that she was such a big part in my maintaining it because she was just so kind and friendly and played along with my juvenile game, and she inspired me and I looked forward to seeing her each day, and Charlie Brown had completely taken over my persona as I sighed to myself from deep inside my gut, "Oh good grief…"

But the Redhead's deep, dark eyes glistened as they locked with mine and she delivered the warmest smile that I'd ever experienced (all things considered…) as she was tugged away by her big Labrador. I thought that time had frozen solid, and I'd stolen too many minutes of this woman's precious time, when, in actuality, it was probably no more than a few seconds that I'd robbed her of, as she loped off behind the dog, turning back slightly as she queried, "So, watcha got?"

Me- I GO TO PIECES (Peter & Gordon) played in my ears as I came around…
Her- THAT'S THE WAY GOD PLANNED IT (Billy Preston)

Indeed.

Off I wandered toward home. Music, and all its meaning, had eluded me. All I really wanted was to try to grasp some small amount of the memory of that drastic encounter…the way she looked, mostly, but alas, it was no more than a dreadful blur. Details about her seemed somehow pointless as I now became consumed with my boyish foolishness and dreary demeanor in the presence of this pretty stranger. Perhaps the music would heal me again somehow, if I could sort out my priorities in all of this mess.

Day 42-

Another fitful night of sleep would precede my dressing out for my walk. By the time I hit the boulevard, I felt out of place. Even as I passed the regulars, I hardly fathomed what might be in store until I spied a tall, slender young lady walking toward me that I immediately recognized as Frenchie.

I was acutely aware of the Isley Brothers in my ears wailing on, "Who's That Lady," and being slightly perplexed as to why I even had that song in my library at all, as she drew nearer and started to hang her head a bit and move over to the side of the path when I pointed at her earphones and called out my now-trademark "What's on the box?" eagerly anticipating some sort of fresh response that might make me forget all about the Redhead. Her reaction was as if she had just come under attack by a swarm of gnats as she batted her head and dark hair all about and blushed through numerous hues from solid red to pink. She was largely embarrassed as she barely uttered any semblance of vocabulary and simply kept her stride right past me. "Fucking train wreck" was all I could mutter to myself as a dark cloud of depression began to set in over me, and I silently wished that we'd never cross paths again.

No sooner had the cloud gathered when a ray of sunshine broke it up as I looked down the road at the Redhead. I felt myself breaking into a nervous smile, but a smile nonetheless, as I braced for the worst, and as if the day before had never happened I threw out...

Me- I FALL TO PIECES (Patsy Cline)
Her- STOP BREAKING DOWN (The Rolling Stones)

Yessss...All was well in the universe when the next song to pop into my head was the Talking Heads, "Once In A Lifetime"; yes, indeed, *"same as it ever was."*

Day 43-

Totally back in a good way and off an' walkin', I went, and not too long into it, I could see a statuesque but wimpy sort of a silhouette ahead and determined immediately that it was not the Redhead. It was Frenchie, and it was not really a bad thing as she was pleasant on the eyes in a beautifully dorky sort of way, and I was feeling a tad pleasant at the sight of her. She approached me with her head held high and bopping along to whatever was going through her earpods when she smiled ever so widely and blurted out, "WHAT ARE YOU DOIN' IN MY LIFE," Tom Petty And The Heartbreakers! and just waltzed right on by as proud as a peacock.

Whoa!! What was that?!? I wondered in a stunned yet positive flash. Now the coin drops, and she gets a dial tone?! I had nothin', I thought, and I just had to let it go, and I guess my silence and lack of response spoke volumes for me. It was cool. Really, it was. But while it seemed to be her way of saying, "I get it," it was sort of too little too late, and if there's anything that I'd learned in my rather uneventful life, it was that any time someone tells you, "I get it," they don't. So my strolling continued with my last thought toward her being, "no harm, no foul."

It's just that I seemed to be needing a good comeback dose of the gal with the fiery hair and the great range of musical taste that I'd come to know. I was back on the music now, at least with her. That's all it seemed to be anyway, and that's when I saw her coming up ahead.

Me- OWNER OF A LONELY HEART (Yes)

Her- I'LL ONLY BREAK YOUR HEART (Holly Williams) with this later…

Me- BAD LIVER AND A BROKEN HEART (Hayes Carll)

Her- ONE FOR MY BABY (AND ONE MORE FOR THE ROAD) (Rob Wasserman)

Day 44-

Me- OPEN YOUR HEART (Madonna)

Her- HANGIN' UP MY HEART (Emmylou Harris + Rodney Crowell)

And again…

Me- BETWEEN HEAVEN AND HELL (Hank Williams Jr.)

Her- STUCK IN THE MIDDLE WITH YOU (The Jeff Healey Band)

Day 45-

Me- HEAVEN HELP THE FOOL (Bob Weir)

Her- GO STRAIGHT TO HELL (The Clash) followed around by…

Me- RUN LIKE HELL (Pink Floyd)

Her- FROM HELL TO PARADISE (The Mavericks)

Day 46-

Me- I CAN RUN WITH THE BIG DOGS (Waylon Jennings)

Her- I WON'T RUN NO MORE (Social Distortion) next lap…

Me- NO ONE TO RUN WITH (The Allman Brothers Band)

Her- LONG MAY YOU RUN (Neil Young)

Day 47-

Sunday morning rolled around, and after a month and a half of this health kick and my wife seeing the affect it was having on me, she decided that she wanted to tag along and get some striding going with me and share the fitness and fresh air. I was more than pleased to have her join me and never gave a second thought to the Redhead and just naturally left my iPod in my room as it would have been kind of rude...Yet when we started out together, I couldn't help but wonder what may play out.

The two of us managed to talk up a storm and catch up on all matters of our lives when about halfway through our stroll, the Redhead came galloping toward us with that large Labrador, and instantly my wife dropped her line of conversation to exclaim that "this was just the type of dog she really wanted to get and get soon, and maybe I could look into getting her one this coming Christmas and..." when the Fiery One passed by looking up at me and shouting out, "I'VE GOT YOU UNDER MY SKIN" (Frank Sinatra).

Yeah!! I blasted back at her as she breezed on by us, knowing she understood I had no weapon with which to return fire, and I probably looked a bit awkward saying so. So cool, I thought. But the wife was thinking something altogether different and quickly tossed a "What was that all about?" at me.

I simply offered that she was a regular and that was how I "rolled" with my fellow music lovers out here on the walking path...That seemed to work just fine as she went right back to the subject of us, well, her, getting a big dog. Like that yellow Lab. Like that redhead's.

Day 48-

Me- I GUESS WE SHOULDN'T TALK ABOUT THAT NOW (Bettye LaVette)

Her- GIRLS TALK (Dave Edmunds) with…

Me- PLEASE DON'T TALK ABOUT ME WHEN I'M GONE (Leon Redbone)

Her- EVERYBODY'S TALKIN' (Harry Nilsson)

Day 49-

Me- TALKIN' 'BOUT YOU (The Rolling Stones)

Her- YOU TALK TOO MUCH (George Thorogood And The Destroyers) then…

Me- LET ME TALK TO YOU (Waylon Jennings)

Her- YOUR MIND IS ON VACATION (AND YOUR MOUTH IS WORKING OVERTIME) (Van Morrison)

Day 50-

Me- LEAVIN' ON A JET PLANE (Peter, Paul and Mary)

Her- SHUT UP AND GET ON THE PLANE (The Drive-By Truckers) and…

Me- YOU'RE NOT ALONE ANYMORE (The Traveling Wilburys)

Her- ALONE IN THE DARK (John Hiatt)

And after those first 50 days without smoking and playing along with this rather intriguing young lady, the next 73 days went something like this…

Me- CRY ME A RIVER (Joe Cocker)

Her- MANY RIVERS TO CROSS (Jimmy Cliff) with this to follow…

Me- CRY BABY CRY (The Beatles)

Her- BIG GIRLS DON'T CRY (Frankie Valli And The Four Seasons)

Me- OCEAN OF NOISE (Arcade Fire)

Her- DROWNED (The Who)

Me- BIG LOVE (Little Village)

Her- LITTLE HEAD (John Hiatt)

Me- HE'LL HAVE TO GO (Elvis Presley)

Her- SURE DIDN'T TAKE HER LONG (Waylon Jennings)

Me- I'M FREE (The Rolling Stones)

Her- SLAVE (The Rolling Stones)

Me- WISH YOU WERE HERE (Fleetwood Mac)

Her- SHE'S NOT THERE (The Zombies)

Me- MONEY (Pink Floyd)

Her- CAN'T BUY ME LOVE (The Beatles)

Me- WAITING FOR THE WORLD TO TURN AROUND (Lucinda Williams)

Her- WE LIVE IN TWO DIFFERENT WORLDS (Tompall Glaser)

Me- SITTIN' ON TOP OF THE WORLD (The Grateful Dead)

Her- WORLD TURNING (Fleetwood Mac)

Me- SLEEPLESS NIGHTS (Gram Parsons)
Her- SLEEPWALKER (The Kinks)

Me- HAVE A LITTLE FAITH IN ME (John Hiatt)
Her- HAVE MERCY (Phish)

Me- HEY JOE (Jimi Hendrix)
Her- JOE MAMA (Fishwacker)

Me- SWEET MAMA (Billy Joe Shaver)
Her- SOMEBODY'S MAMA (Joe Nichols)

Me- ROLL ON BIG MAMA (Joe Stampley And Moe Bandy)
Her- NACHO MAMA (Joe Ely)

Me- THESE ARE DAYS (10,000 Maniacs)
Her- DAYS GO BY (Keith Urban)

Me- MY BABE (The Righteous Brothers)
Her- IT AIN'T ME BABE (Bob Dylan)

Me- I GOT YOU BABA (Sonny And Cher)
Her- BABE I'M GONNA LEAVE YOU (Led Zeppelin)

Me- PAINT IT BLACK (The Rolling Stones)
Her- WHEN I PAINT MY MASTERPIECE (The Band)

Me- WIN, LOSE OR DRAW (The Allman Brothers Band)
Her- YOU WIN AGAIN (Martina McBride)

Me- I'LL LOVE YOU AS MUCH AS I CAN (Billy Joe Shaver)
Her- HONEY DON'T (The Beatles)

Me- OUR HOUSE (Crosby, Stills & Nash)
Her- BURNIN' DOWN THE HOUSE (Talking Heads)

Me- THIEF IN THE NIGHT (The Rolling Stones)
Her- ROB YOU BLIND (Driftwater)

Me- WHAT DO YOU WANT FROM ME? (Pink Floyd)
Her- NOTHING IS GOOD ENOUGH (Aimee Mann) along
    with...
Me- WHAT WAS IT THAT YOU WANTED? (Willie Nelson)
Her- NOTHING FROM NOTHING (Billy Preston)

Me- COME TOGETHER (The Beatles)
Her- GO IT ALONE (Jason Isbell) and...
Me- COME WITH ME (Waylon Jennings)
Her- BEAT IT (Michael Jackson)

Me- NEVER SAY DIE (Waylon Jennings)
Her- NEVER MY LOVE (The Association)

Me- WHO KNOWS? (The Zac Brown Band)
Her- HEAVEN ONLY KNOWS (Emmylou Harris)

Me- THE KIND OF PLACE (Jerry Joseph)
Her- I DON'T WANT TO BE (Bo Bice)

Me- GOIN' DOWN THE ROAD (FEELIN' BAD) (The Grateful
    Dead)
Her- DRIVE SOUTH (John Hiatt) and with that...
Me- IF LOVING YOU IS WRONG (Cassandra Wilson)
Her- WRONG WAY FEELING (Bob Weir)

Me- INCENSE AND PEPPERMINTS (Strawberry Alarm Clock)
Her- WIGGLES AND RITALIN (Reckless Kelly)

Me- WHO WERE YOU THINKIN' OF? (The Texas Tornados)
Her- KNIGHTS IN WHITE SATIN (The Moody Blues)

Me- I CAN TELL YOU WHAT YOU WANT (The Jagged Frequency)
Her- HOW WOULD YOU KNOW? (Big Wreck)

Me- IF YOU WERE MINE TO LOSE (Waylon Jennings)
Her- LOSER (The Grateful Dead)

Me- WHEN CAN I SEE YOU? (Babyface)
Her- WHEN I'M GONE (Phil Ochs)

Me- ROLL WITH THE CHANGES (REO Speedwagon)
Her- ROLL ON (J. J. Cale)

Me- CAN'T YOU SEE? (The Marshal Tucker Band)
Her- I'D RATHER GO BLIND (Etta James)

Me- LOUISIANA MAN (Doug Kershaw)
Her- MISSISSIPPI QUEEN (Mountain)

Me- WHERE IS THE LOVE? (Black Eyed Peas)
Her- OVER YONDER (Steve Earle)

Me- YOU WERE ALWAYS HAPPY (Spearmint)
Her- TILL THERE WAS YOU (The Beatles)

Me- HOW MUCH IS ENOUGH? (Bad Religion)
Her- I CAN'T BE SATISFIED (Dale Watson)

Me- YOU'VE GOT ANOTHER (Drive-By Truckers)
Her- THE OTHER ONE (The Grateful Dead) followed by…
Me- THE SAME THING (Muddy Waters)
Her- WHICH ONE? (Chris Brown)

Me- WASTIN' TIME (Waylon Jennings)
Her- I AIN'T WASTIN' TIME NO MORE (The Allman Brothers)

Me- WHO ARE YOU? (The Who)
Her- YOU DON'T KNOW ME (Ray Charles)

Me- GOD GAVE ME YOU (Blake Shelton)
Her- DROPKICK ME JESUS (Bobby Bare) then…
Me- JESUS ON A GREYHOUND (Shelby Lynne)
Her- HOLY ROLLER (Oh Susanna) and even one more time that
   day…
Me- GOD (John Lennon)
Her- JUST WANNA SEE HIS FACE (The Rolling Stones)

Me- WHO COULD WANT MORE? (Lee Michaels)
Her- I DO (Toya)

Me- PAPA WAS A ROLLIN' STONE (The Temptations)
Her- TELL MAMA (Savoy Brown)

Me- IT TAKES TWO (Katy Perry)
Her- I'M ONE (The Who) and on the next trip…
Me- ONE (U2)
Her- ONE IS THE LONELIEST NUMBER (The Product)

Me- HOW DO YOU FEEL? (The Jefferson Airplane)
Her- I FEEL FINE (The Beatles)

Me- VOODOO CHILD (Jimi Hendrix)
Her- I PUT A SPELL ON YOU (Creedence Clearwater Revival)

Me- DON'T YOU LIE TO ME (The Blasters)
Her- TELL ME LIES (Ashley Tisdale)

Me- TELL THE TRUTH (Derek And The Dominos)
Her- ALL YOU EVER DO IS BRING ME DOWN (The Mavericks)

Me- YOU CAN STILL CHANGE YOUR MIND (Tom Petty + The Heartbreakers)
Her- A CHANGE IS GONNA COME (The Band) returned with…
Me- CHANGES (David Bowie)
Her- THINGS HAVE CHANGED (Bob Dylan)

Me- YOU MAKE ME LIVE (Isaac Hayes)
Her- LIVE AND LET DIE (Paul McCartney)

Me- HEAVEN OR HELL (Waylon Jennings)
Her- PURGATORY LINE (Drive-By Truckers)

Me- WHY? (Avril Lavigne)
Her- BECAUSE (The Dave Clark Five)

Me- FOUR STRONG WINDS (Neil Young)
Her- BLOW AWAY (The Grateful Dead)

Me- PLEASE DON'T LET ME BE MISUNDERSTOOD (The Animals)
Her- MR. MISUNDERSTOOD (Eric Church)

Me- I LEFT MY HEART IN SAN FRANCISCO (Tony Bennett)
Her- KEEP LOOKING (Sade)

Me- RAMBLIN' GAMBLIN' MAN (Bob Seger)
Her- RAMBLE ON (Led Zeppelin)

Me- AROUND THE BEND (Joe Bonamassa)
Her- SLOW TURNING (John Hiatt)

Me- IT ONLY HURTS ME WHEN I CRY (Dwight Yoakam)
Her- CRY BABY CRY (The Beatles)

Me- COME PICK ME UP (Ryan Adams)
Her- IT'S TOO LATE (Derek And The Dominos)

Me- LAWMAN (The Jefferson Airplane)
Her- I FOUGHT THE LAW (Bobby Fuller Four)

Me- INTERSTATE LOVE SONG (Stone Temple Pilots)
Her- HIGHWAY TO HELL (AC/DC)

Me- CRY TILL MY TEARS RUN DRY (Linda Ronstadt)
Her- CRY ME A RIVER (Joe Cocker)

Me- IT HURTS ME TOO (The Grateful Dead)
Her- IT DON'T HURT (Sheryl Crow) and then came...
Me- IT WON'T HURT (Dwight Yoakam)
Her- I DON'T HURT ANYMORE (Martina McBride)

Me- EVERYBODY'S GOT SOMETHING TO HIDE EXCEPT FOR
    ME AND MY MONKEY (The Beatles)
Her- TOO MUCH MONKEY BUSINESS (Chuck Berry)

Me- ONE MORE TIME (John Hiatt)
Her- OUT OF TIME (The Rolling Stones) coming back around...
Me- TIME HAS COME TODAY (The Chambers Brothers)
Her- TIME WAITS FOR NO ONE (The Rolling Stones)

Me- FRACTION TOO MUCH FRICTION (Tim Finn)
Her- SPARKS WILL FLY (The Rolling Stones)

Me- HOLD ON TIGHT (Electric Light Orchestra)
Her- RELEASE ME (Johnny Adams)

Me- ONLY DADDY THAT'LL WALK THE LINE (Waylon Jennings)
Her- WALK IT OFF (Toby Keith) on the second go 'round...
Me- I CAN'T WALK THIS TIME (Ry Cooder)
Her- WALK LIKE A MAN (Frankie Valli And The Four Seasons)

Me- I WALK THE LINE (Johnny Cash)
Her- WALK RIGHT BACK (The Everly Brothers)

Me- BROKEN DOWN COWBOY (John Fogerty)
Her- BLAME IT ON WAYLON (Josh Thompson)

Me- DO YOU WANT MY JOB? (Little Village)
Her- I DON'T WORK THAT CHEAP (Bill Kirchen)

So...wow! How cool is all this!?!? How great is my world!?!? I mean, it's all so innocent and real and fun and...right!?!? I'm thinkin', I gotta tell my brother Stephen about this because he would dig it! I'm gettin' this vibe, right? I'm like connecting with this woman that I know nothing about except for her love of music! I'm sharing, and she's sharing in response, and that is just cool, and I feel good and life is good. Right?

Day 124-

So I know now that just thinking about ever stopping this woman ever again, or even just hoping that she will slow down, for any reason, like trying to string out this micro-exchange of musical musing for maybe a brief chat about the individual intricacy of it all was never going to happen. I mean, never. Ever. And why would I be that stupid anyway? Right? It was all that I could ask for just to have her play along. And only if and when she wanted to. And for now, it seemed as though she did.

So it went...

Me- SOMETIMES IT TAKES BALLS TO BE WOMAN (Elizabeth Cook)
Her- IF ANYONE'S GOT THE BALLS (I DO) (Eddie Spaghetti)

Day 125-

Me- SLOW MOVIN' OUTLAW (Waylon Jennings)
Her- (IT'S) HARD TO BE AN OUTLAW (ANYMORE) (Willie Nelson + Billy
Joe Shaver)...which led to this on the come-back-around trip...

Me- MY HEROES HAVE ALWAYS BEEN COWBOYS (Waylon Jennings)
Her- ARE THERE ANY MORE REAL COWBOYS? (Neil Young, Willie Nelson)

Day 126-

Me- I WISH I WAS THE MOON (Neko Case)
Her- BAD MOON RISING (Creedence Clearwater Revival)
   along with...
Me- MOONLIGHT MILE (The Rolling Stones)
Her- FORTY MILES OF BAD ROAD (Duane Eddy)

Day 127-

Me- WACO MOON (Jimmie Dale Gilmore)
Her- TEXAS MOON (Stoney LaRue) plus the second time...
Me- YOU HUNG THE MOON (Jessi Colter)
Her- MOONSHADOW (Cat Stevens)

Day 128-

Me- TRY A LITTLE TENDERNESS (Otis Redding)
Her- TRY AND TRY AGAIN (Billy Joe Shaver) then...
Me- TRY (JUST A LITTLE BIT HARDER) (Janis Joplin)
Her- TRYIN' TO OUTRUN THE WIND (Waylon Jennings)

Day 129-

Me- CATCH THE WIND (Donovan)
Her- GONE WITH THE WIND (Rob Wasserman) and later...
Me- AGAINST THE WIND (Bob Seger)
Her- BLACK-THROATED WIND (The Grateful Dead)

Day 130-

Me- DON'T LET THE SUN GO DOWN ON ME (Elton John)
Her- AIN'T NO SUNSHINE (Bill Withers) followed by...
Me- I'LL FOLLOW THE SUN (The Beatles)
Her- THE SUN ALSO SETS (Ryan Adams)

Day 131-

Me- WALK IN THE SUNSHINE (Bob Weir)
Her- THE SUN AIN'T GONNA SHINE ANYMORE (Jay + The Americans)
with this later...
Me- WE'LL SING IN THE SUNSHINE (Gale Garnett)
Her- THERE IS NO SUNSHINE (Jamey Johnson)

Day 132-

Me- YOU ARE MY SUNSHINE (Ray Charles)
Her- WHEN THE SUN GOES DOWN (Joe Bonamassa)

Day 133-

Me- BETTER DAYS (Southside Johnny + The Asbury Jukes)
Her- THE DAY YOU DIE (Lindi Ortega) then there was...
Me- CLOUDY DAYS (Waylon Jennings)
Her- COLD DAY IN JULY (The Dixie Chicks)

Day 134-

Me- DAYS AREN'T LONG ENOUGH (Steve Earle)
Her- DAYS ARE GONE (HAIM) with...
Me- FOUR DAYS OF RAIN (The Flying Burrito Brothers)
Her- EIGHT DAYS A WEEK (The Beatles)

Day 135-

Me- OUT AMONG THE STARS (Waylon Jennings)
Her- FARTHER STARS (John Hiatt) and comin' back...
Me- DARK STAR (The Grateful Dead)
Her- A FALLEN STAR (Ferlin Husky)

Day 136-

Me- EASY STREET (David Lee Roth)
Her- WHERE THE STREETS HAVE NO NAME (U2)

Day 137-

Me- BACK STREET GIRL (The Rolling Stones)
Her- BACK ON THE STREETS AGAIN (Tower Of Power) with
    this...
Me- TAKIN' IT TO THE STREETS (Doobie Brothers)
Her- LONELY STREET (Robby Turner)

Day 138-

Me-LOVE ON A TWO-WAY STREET (The Moments)
Her- POSITIVELY 4th STREET (Bob Dylan) with a few more days
   of...
Me- DANCIN' IN THE STREETS (Martha Reeves + The Vandellas)
Her- TRAMP ON YOUR STREET (Billy Joe Shaver)

Day 139-

Me- ON MAIN STREET (Los Lobos)
Her- STREETS OF LAREDO (Marty Robbins)

Day 140-

Me- STREETS OF BAKERSFIELD (Dwight Yoakam)
Her- STREETS OF BALTIMORE (Gram Parsons)

Day 141-

Me- HEART LIKE MINE (Miranda Lambert)
Her- HEART OF STONE (The Rolling Stones) with second helping of...

Me- CHANGE OF HEART (Tom Petty + The Heartbreakers)
Her- HERE COMES THE HEARTACHE (Jason James)

Day 142-

Me- FEARLESS HEART (Steve Earle)
Her- FOOLISH HEART (The Grateful Dead) and…
Me- CARELESS HEART (Roy Orbison)
Her- COLD, COLD HEART (Hank Williams)

Day 143-

Me- FIRST AND LAST TIME (Billy Joe Shaver)
Her- FIRST LAST CHANCE (Michael Grimm)

Day 144-

Me- TIGHT CONNECTION TO MY HEART (Bob Dylan)
Her- UNCOMMON CONNECTION (John Hiatt)

Day 145-

Me- PRESENT TENSE (Gurf Morlix)
Her- IT'S ALL OVER NOW (The Rolling Stones)

Day 146-

So cool, all this. Woke up happy, as I had for nearly 5 months now, and the first thing to pop into my little head was how much I looked forward to my walk. And just as soon as I hit the big street with the golf course I made out the figure of a lady… striding along but not jogging, and no sign of a dog. It took but a second for her getting closer to realize who she was...Frenchie.

Then it dawned on me that in these last months I had rarely missed a day of seeing the Redhead. Not only that, but when I did, it seemed Frenchie would show up in her place. Then she was upon me with that elegant but calculated stride and her head held high and she let go of a hesitant grin as she looked across at me and presented, "EAT AT HOME " (Paul McCartney). "LATE FOR SUPPER" (Jerry Garcia) I begrudgingly offered in return as she swished on by.

Sheesh. Gimme a break. C'mon, Red, where are ya?

I mean, don't get me wrong. Frenchie was a looker, God knows. But she just didn't get it, I thought. And while both women were attractive, it wasn't about that with the regular gal that I'd trade titles with. Right? It was that, ah, um...connection. Yeah, that was it! And that came to me only because the song now playing through my earpods was, "Connection" by the Rolling Stones. But that connection was not to be had this day and as I came about the last turn in my walk, and apparently Frenchie was too, approaching me again and lifting her finger up to her ear as she came forth with,"GOT TO GET YOU INTO MY LIFE" by the Beatles while I threw back, "GET OUT OF MY LIFE WOMAN" by the Paul Butterfield Blues Band. Sheesh.

Day 147-

Another day and not so great. Started off in a funk as I began the morning jaunt, and it quickly got funkier as I immediately caught sight of Frenchie coming toward me. Screw it, I thought as I let my guard down and managed a smile as she passed by and softly and pleasantly sang out, "LATE FOR CHURCH" (Drive-By Truckers), to which I just as pleasantly returned with,

"LATE FOR MY FUNERAL" (Mike Stinson). Then more bad funk came down as I came to my last turn and caught up with her again to receive, "I WANT TO HOLD YOUR HAND" (The Beatles), and I reciprocated with, "BACK OF MY HAND" (John Hiatt). Red!! Arrggghh!!

Day 148-

It never occurred to me why I was in a bad mood for 3 days running now, but here I was, starting off again and quickly coming up on Frenchie and not even slightly aware of what was coming through my ear lines as she motioned toward her head and let out, "COME A LITTLE BIT CLOSER" by Jay and The Americans to which I could only counter with "DON'T COME AROUND HERE NO MORE," by Tom Petty and The Heartbreakers. Oy.

Thinking that she was never one for two trips like Red and that it wasn't as early as it usually was in my walk, I might miss her at the end today, but…Nooo…"STORMS NEVER LAST" (Jessi Colter), to which I spit back, "LOOKS LIKE RAIN" (Bob Weir). RED!! Can't take anymore! Help!

Day 149-

Salvation finally came the next day, and I can't tell you how happy I was to see my lady friend and her dog trotting toward me, except that I could not muster even a thought later on of Frenchie or the fact that she had not managed another appearance to ruin my life again. So I did what I had to do as the young gal approached…

Me- WITH OR WITHOUT YOU (U2)
Her- ONE OF THE FORTUNATE FEW (Delbert McClinton)

Ahh…so good.

Day 150-

Me- UNCHAIN MY HEART (Ray Charles)
Her- SLAVE TO LOVE (Bryan Ferry) followed by…
Me- LET'S NOT SAY GOODBYE (Raul Malo)
Her- LET'S SAY GOOD NIGHT (Los Lobos)

Day 151-

Me- HEARTACHE TONIGHT (The Eagles)
Her- TONIGHT THE HEARTACHE'S ON ME (The Dixie Chicks)

Day 152-

Me- IF I GIVE MY SOUL (Shaver)
Her- SOUL SACRIFICE (Santana) returning with…
Me- PLUNDERED MY SOUL (The Rolling Stones)
Her- SOUL SURVIVOR (The Rolling Stones)

Day 153-

Me- JUMP (FOR MY LOVE) (The Pointer Sisters)
Her- JUMP BACK (Kingfish) along with…
Me- JUMP AROUND (House Of Pain)
Her- JUMP INTO THE FIRE (Harry Nilsson)

Day 154-

Me- WALK DON'T RUN (The Ventures)
Her- WALK AWAY (Joe Walsh)

Day 155-

Me- FROM HANK TO HENDRIX (Neil Young)
Her- ARE YOU SURE HANK DONE IT THIS WAY? (Waylon Jennings)

Day 156-

Me- POUR SOME SUGAR ON ME (Def Leppard)
Her- SWEET DREAMS (Patsy Cline)

Day 157-

Me- NOTHING ELSE MATTERS (David Garret)
Her- IT DOESN'T MATTER ANYMORE (Buddy Holly) and then
    came…
Me- SHINE A LIGHT (The Rolling Stones)
Her- TURN OUT MY LIGHTS (Justin Townes Earle)

Day 158-

Me- I KNEW YOU WERE WAITING (FOR ME) (Aretha Franklin)
Her-I KNEW YOU'D BE LEAVING (Waylon Jennings)

Day 159-

Me- HOW DO YOU LIKE ME NOW? (Toby Keith)
Her- I THINK I'M GONNA KILL MYSELF (Waylon Jennings)

Day 160-

Me- GIVE A LITTLE BIT (Supertramp)
Her- GIVE IT UP (John Hiatt)

Day 161-

Me- EVERYTHING IS BROKEN (Bob Dylan)
Her- YOU CAN'T FIX THIS (Stevie Nicks + Dave Grohl)

Day 162-

Me- WAITING ON THE WORLD TO CHANGE (John Mayer)
Her- WHERE WERE YOU (WHEN THE WORLD STOPPED TURNING?) (Alan Jackson) and then there was...
Me- I BEEN ALL AROUND THIS WORLD (The Grateful Dead)
Her- BEFORE THE WORLD WAS BIG (Girlpool)

Day 163-

Me- BOTH SIDES NOW (Joni Mitchell)
Her- THE OTHER SIDE (Ryan Bingham) then on the next trip...
Me- HOW BAD'S THE COFFEE? (John Hiatt)
Her- HOW BAD DO YOU WANT IT? (Don Henley)

Day 164-

Me- I'M YOUR PUPPET (James and Bobby Purify)
Her- I'VE GOT NO STRINGS (Gypsy Kings)

Day 165-

Me- A THING ABOUT YOU (Tom Petty + The Heartbreakers)
Her- ALL THINGS MUST PASS (George Harrison)

Day 166-

Me- IS THERE ANYBODY OUT THERE? (Pink Floyd)
Her- NOBODY HOME (Pink Floyd) followed back around
    with...
Me- STAND BY ME (Ry Cooder)
Her- YOU'RE STILL STANDING THERE (Steve Earle)

Day 167-

Me- GET UP, STAND UP (Bob Marley + The Wailers)
Her- SURE AS I'M SITTIN' HERE (John Hiatt)

Day 168-

Me- STARTING ALL OVER (Israel Kamakawiwo'ole)
Her- NOT A SECOND TIME (The Beatles) then came…
Me- ENCHANTED (Stevie Nicks)
Her- DISGUSTED (Lucinda Williams)

Day 169-

Me- IF YOU LIVED HERE, YOU'D BE HOME (Emmylou Harris)
Her- HOME FOR SALE (Dwight Yoakam)

Day 170-

Me- HOLDING THINGS TOGETHER (Merle Haggard)
Her- HOLDIN' MY OWN (Eric Church)

Day 171-

Me- REMEMBERING (Ashley Campbell)
Her- HOW TO FORGET (Jason Isbell) then came back with…
Me- DON'T FORGET TO REMEMBER ME (Carrie Underwood)
Her- UNFORGETTABLE (Nat "King" Cole)

Day 172-

Me- I GO WILD (The Rolling Stones)
Her- WILD AND LONESOME (Shooter Jennings + Patty Griffin)

Day 173-

Me- I AIN'T LIVIN' LONG LIKE THIS (Emmylou Harris)
Her- I FOUND THE BODY (Fenixon)

Day 174-

Me- I KNEW THE BRIDE (WHEN SHE USED TO ROCK & ROLL)
    (Dave Edmunds)
Her- THE GROOM'S STILL WAITING AT THE ALTAR (Bob
    Dylan)

Day 175-

Me- HAD ENOUGH? (Tom Gillam)
Her- HAD IT WITH YOU (The Rolling Stones)

Day 176-

Me- HERE IS WHAT IS (Daniel Lanois)
Her- HERE THERE AND EVERYWHERE (The Beatles)
Awesome. Perfect. Man, I gotta tell my brother Stephen about
    all this. He would love this stuff.

Day 177-

Six months. No cigarettes. And, certainly, no regrets. And no
bad days, really. Yeah, I wanted to tell my brother about this little
game I was playing with a stranger. A fiery, redheaded stranger

(and right there, was another song, a Willie Nelson song, "The Redheaded Stranger"), no less. He would truly be intrigued as I was with the repertoire of artists that she was coming up with on a daily basis, many of them his favorites (like The Stones, U2, Prince, The Clash, hell, even Waylon and The Dead). But she surprised me as well. And as much as Stephen would have likely wanted more details about the young woman, I was just happy with the musical playfulness of it all. Yes, I was still in love with my wife and even seemed to get along great with her now that I'd quit the Marlboros once again. I didn't stink up my surroundings with that offensive secondhand tobacco smoke.

I also looked forward to seeing my wife each day and believed that she was much happier in seeing me. Still, I looked forward to the honest, innocent repartee with the walker/jogger and the absence of any mind games or social-emotional psychological garbage that might have accompanied all this.

No read-between-the-lines, ulterior, subconscious bullshit.

Right?

Then this happened…

Day 178-

The day began pretty much like all the rest. The weather was nice. My slate of chores and errands had been cleared, and I was off, without really much of a care for anything but to see Red and discover what was in the rotation of our playlists. The stars and planets all seemed to come into alignment as I spied her coming at me from up the road and my mental gears shifted into cognitive awareness of what was going through my ears while I ever so slightly held my breath in anticipation of what her return would be.

Then I froze. Mentally. Oh, I was still walking, putting one now very clumsy foot in front of the other, but I was going into that nitrous oxide narco-numb blaze like I did the first few times I saw this lady. She was getting closer, and suddenly, I was really making out all the glorious physical features of this woman like I never had before, like, her eyes, that were dark and beautiful, and burning right into mine, as if she could, and was—because now my throat had lost all moisture and my tongue was limp and the cerebral synapses just weren't firing quite as they should...

It was a Rolling Stones song that was loudly banging between my two ears, and I was feelin' it! I mean, I was FEELING IT!

The band was going to introduce it to the world on *The Ed Sullivan Show* (at least, this is how I had heard the story went), and for those of you that are too young to know, the program was a primetime, family entertainment hour with a rather conservative host. It was he that would not allow the band to perform it on nationwide TV with its original title and lyrics. Now, trust me, today, it would have been considered tame, and perhaps even juvenile. Low key. Lame. But that was then, and this is now, and...I still somehow couldn't shout out to a passing female "friend," "Hey, let's go to bed together"!! Could I?? Well, like I said, I was feelin' it. So...I did.

Fuck it. And even with other folks nearby and within an earshot, I shouted—

Me- LET'S SPEND THE NIGHT TOGETHER (The Rolling Stones)
Her- IN YOUR WILDEST DREAMS (The Moody Blues)

Wow!! Boom!! That just happened!! What?!? Yeah!! Right!! I mean, right?? I mean, what just happened?? Holy shit. She never batted an eyelash, she never missed a beat. And, she never missed a step. That was it, and she was gone.

I had gotten what I'd hoped for, but for the first time, I felt kinda like a turd, and I didn't really know why. It didn't seem to bother her the way it felt like it was bothering me. Was I missing something? I mean, was it just some weird, cosmic occurrence that had no meaning, just the norm? Just the status quo? Same as it ever was?

I did not see her again that morning, so I just assumed she had gotten an earlier start than me or maybe just cut short her routine. As I walked along I started to think about it even more. Everything. The whole sequence of the morning's passing, how this all started, what it did for me (or to me?), and how this sort of interaction had come to a point of minds intertwining with casual, split-second mental incidents...

Nah, I finally let myself think as I let it go and looked down the street toward home and forward to what the next day or time might bring.

And the next 49 days went something like this...

Me- FRIEND OF THE DEVIL (The Grateful Dead)
Her- SYMPATHY FOR THE DEVIL (The Rolling Stones) followed
    up with...
Me- TAKE IT AS IT COMES (The Rowans)
Her- TAKE ANOTHER LOOK (Little Village)

Me- PANTIES IN YOUR PURSE (The Drive-by Truckers)
Her- THAT'S WHAT GIRLS DO (No Secrets) along with...
Me- THE LAST SONG I WILL WRITE (Jason Isbell)
Her- A MOST DISGUSTING SONG (Rodriguez)

Me- LAID (James)
Her- THEN AGAIN (Court Yard Hounds)

Me- PLEASE DON'T TELL ME HOW THE STORY ENDS (Kris Kristofferson)
Her- PLEASE GO HOME (The Rolling Stones)

Me- THE OTHER SIDE OF TOWN (Steve Earle)
Her- BUTTHOLEVILLE (The Drive-by Truckers) and then came...
Me- SHAME ON YOU (Willie Nelson)
Her- SHAME ON ME The Bottle Rockets)

Me- THE MESS WE'RE IN (Los Lobos)
Her- MOST MESSED UP (The Old 97's) and then...
Me- WAITING FOR A FRIEND (The Rolling Stones)
Her- WAITING FOR A MIRACLE (The Jerry Garcia Band)

Me- YOU TOOK ME BY SURPRISE (Jessi Colter)
Her- SURPRISE, SURPRISE (The Rolling Stones)

Me- SCREWTOPIA (The Drive-by Truckers)
Her- SCREW YOU, WE'RE FROM TEXAS (Ray Wylie Hubbard)

Me- SUPERSTAR (Raul Malo)
Her- SUPER FREAK (Rick James)

Me- LIES (The Rolling Stones)
Her- UGLY TRUTH (Lucinda Williams)

Me- UNDER YOUR SPELL AGAIN (Waylon Jennings + Jessi Colter)
Her- UNDER MY THUMB (The Rolling Stones)

Me- YOU GOT ANOTHER (The Drive-by Truckers)
Her- YOU GOT IT (Roy Orbison)

Me- YOU DON'T KNOW SHIT ABOUT LOVE (Hotflash)
Her- WHAT'S LOVE GOT TO DO WITH IT? (Tina Turner)

Me- ALL I REALLY WANNA DO (The Byrds)
Her- YOU DON'T HAVE TO MEAN IT (The Rolling Stones)

Me- GIMME A SGN (Ryan Adams)
Her- DOOM AND GLOOM (The Rolling Stones)

Me- THE DOOR IS ALWAYS OPEN (Waylon Jennings)
Her- DON'T YOU WISH IT WAS TRUE? (John Fogerty)

Me- GETTING BETTER (The Beatles)
Her- IT HASN'T HAPPENED YET (John Hiatt)

Me- IT DON'T GET ANY BETTER THAN THIS (George Jones)
Her- IT ALL ENDS NOW (James Newton Howard)

Me- HOW DO YOU KEEP LOVE ALIVE? (Ryan Adams)
Her- KILL YOU (Eminem)

Me- EVERLASTING LOVE (Carl Carlton)
Her- NO SUCH THING (Dwight Yoakam)

Me- HOW FAR CAN I FALL? (Lindy Gravelle)
Her- ROCK BOTTOM (Dickey Betts Band)

Me- CONVERSATION WITH THE DEVIL (Ray Wylie Hubbard)
Her- DEVIL'S WAITIN' (Black Rebel Motorcycle Club)

Me- EVERY PART OF ME (Steve Earle)
Her- NO GOOD FOR ME (Waylon Jennings) and then came...
Me- EVERYBODY PLAYS THE FOOL (The Main Ingredient)
Her- EVERYBODY'S BITCH (O.L.D.)

Me- WOULDN'T IT MAKE A LOVELY PHOTOGRAPH (Ray LaMontagne)
Her- EVERY PICTURE TELLS A STORY (Rod Stewart)

Me- (I'M GONNA WRITE) A TEAR-STAINED LETTER (Johnny Cash)
Her- TEAR IT UP (Mick Fleetwood's Zoo)

Me- THE WINNER (Kris Kristofferson)
Her- WINNER AT A LOSING GAME (Rascal Flatts)

Me- WE'LL MEET AGAIN (Johnny Cash)
Her- WISH I'D NEVER MET YOU (The Rolling Stones)

Me- TELL ME WHAT YOU SEE (The Beatles)
Her- DON'T TURN AROUND (Doug Sahm) followed up by...
Me- DON'T TRY TO FIGHT IT (Little Tony)
Her- DON'T MIND IF I DID (The Elvin Bishop Band) with a third appearance that day I got...
Me- DON'T THINK I DON'T THINK ABOUT IT (Darius Rucker)
Her- DON'T THINK TWICE IT'S ALL RIGHT (Bob Dylan)

Me- DON'T TOUCH ME THERE (The Tubes)
Her- DON'T TOUCH ME (Tammy Wynette) along with...
Me- TOUCH ME IN THE MORNING (Diana Ross)
Her- I TOUCH MYSELF (The Divinyls)

Me- READY TO GO (Republica)
Her- READY TO RUN (The Dixie Chicks)

Me- I THINK I'M GONNA KILL MYSELF (Waylon Jennings)
Her- SUICIDE IS PAINLESS (Johnny Mandel)

Me- HOW DO YOU LIKE ME NOW?! (Toby Keith)
Her- HOW LONG HAVE YOU BEEN THERE? (Waylon Jennings)
    with...
Me- AIN'T NO REST FOR THE WICKED (Cage The Elephant)
Her- HOW DO YOU SLEEP? (John Lennon)

Me- LOOK WHAT THE CAT DRAGGED IN (The Rolling Stones)
Her- IT IS WHAT IT IS (The Highwaymen)

Me- SOMEHOW, SOMEDAY (Ryan Adams)
Her- SOMEDAY NEVER COMES (John Fogerty)

Me- I SCARE MYSELF (Dan Hicks + His Hot Licks)
Her- SAME THING HAPPENED TO ME (John Prine)

Me- TURN ME ON (Nina Simone)
Her- TURN ME LOOSE (Loverboy)

Me- TELL ME WHAT YOU SEE (The Beatles)
Her- OLD TIMER'S DISEASE (Patterson Hood)

Me- DESIRE (U2)
Her- DESPERATION (Judith Hill)

Me- FOR WHOM THE BELL TOLLS (Metallica)
Her- FOR YOU (Raul Malo)

Me- HEY, HEY, WHAT CAN I DO? (Led Zeppelin)
Her- ACT NATURALLY (The Beatles)

Me- HERE YOU COME AGAIN (Dolly Parton)
Her- HERE WE GO AGAIN (Ray Charles) then came…
Me- HERE I AM (Jessi Colter)
Her- OH NO, NOT YOU AGAIN (The Rolling Stones)

Me- RAGGED BUT RIGHT (Waylon Jennings)
Her- RAGGED AS THE ROAD (Reckless Kelly)

Me- I'VE GOTTA GET A MESSAGE TO YOU (The Bee Gees)
Her- RETURN TO SENDER (Elvis Presley)

Me- SOME DAYS YOU GOTTA DANCE (The Dixie Chicks)
Her- WHEN THE RADIO GOES DEAD (Shooter Jennings + Hierophant)

Me- WHENEVER KINDNESS FAILS (Robert Earl Keen)
Her- WHEN THE PIN HITS THE SHELL (The Drive-by Truckers)

Me- TRY NOT TO LOOK SO PRETTY (Dwight Yoakam)
Her- NEVER HAD A CHANCE (Reckless Kelly)

Me- STARTING TO HURT (Ryan Adams)
Her- (IT) AIN'T KILLED ME YET (Eric Church)

Me- WON'T GET FOOLED AGAIN (The Who)
Her- MAYBE YOU SHOULD'VE BEEN LISTENING (Jessi Colter)

Me- I'VE BEEN WAITING (Little Steven + The Disciples of Soul)
Her- SINCE WHEN? (Raul Malo)

Me- WE'RE GOING WRONG (Cream)
Her- WE'RE ALRIGHT NOW (John Hiatt)

Me- WE USED TO WAIT (Arcade Fire)
Her- WE STAYED TOO LONG (James Newton Howard)

Me- WE CAN WORK IT OUT (The Beatles)
Her- WE'RE NOT GONNA TAKE IT (The Who) juiced up later
    with…
Me- WE STAND A CHANCE (Tom Petty + The Heartbreakers)
Her- WE CAN'T MAKE IT HERE (James McMurtry)

Me- WE REALLY SHOULDN'T BE DOING THIS (George Strait)
Her- THIS IS WHY WE FIGHT (The Decemberists)

Me- WE'LL MEET AGAIN (Johnny Cash)
Her- IF YOU'RE GOING THROUGH HELL (Rodney Atkins)

Me- I RUN TO YOU (Lady Antebellum)
Her- YOU SHOULD HAVE SEEN ME RUNNING (The New
    Riders of the Purple Sage)

Me- ONCE I WAS (Tim Buckley)
Her- FLIRTIN' WITH DISASTER (Molly Hatchet)

Day 240-

Officially 8 months without a smoke and about 229 days into this game of tossing song titles back and forth with a stranger, but who's counting, and she was, after all, a pretty decent looking stranger. But my day began early, about three in the morning...I couldn't sleep, and my thoughts all revolved around the redheaded woman and the encounters of the last month, since shouting out to her, "Let's Spend the Night Together," and her response of, "In Your Wildest Dreams."...Nothin' to it, right? I mean, just a game, nothing more, right? And later on I got this...

Me- NOT THAT FUNNY (Fleetwood Mac)
Her- LAUGH, LAUGH (The Beau Brummels) with a second helping of...
Me- YOU NEVER EVEN CALLED ME BY MY NAME (David Allan Coe)
Her- ASSHOLE(S) (The Drive-by Truckers) and thirds of...
Me- TELL ME HOW YOU LIKE IT (Florida Georgia Line)
Her- UP AGAINST THE WALL, REDNECK MOTHER (Jerry Jeff Walker)

Hmm...

Are my wires crossed? Am I getting some sort of mixed signals? Just as soon (well, about a month or so) as I'd felt I was reading way too much into all this and then reassuring myself that I wasn't, I was now quite confused.

It was all about the music. Just a couple of music lovers, passing like two ships in the night. Every day. Unknowingly blowing their foghorns in the mist. Sharing like interests, but in an effort to keep it simple, cordial, as well as clipped, we'd narrowed it down simply to song titles. Not the lyrics, or the nts. Not the words. Just the titles, ma'am.

ked on back home, and I remained confused and very much in deep, troubled thought long into that day and night, and tossed and turned into the next early morning.

I found myself harkening back to memories of when it all began. It had started with me posing the question first; what's on the box? But I guess from that moment on, I was just happy to get any sort of response, happy that she was gamin' with me. Whether it was positive or negative never really fell into play. I had only made myself aware of what was playing in my ears so that I had a ball to serve into her court for her to return, and just let the volleying happen innocently. Playfully. Platonically. Jeez, why would I waste my time otherwise? Yeah, she was pretty and all. But I never had any conscious intentions. It was just good fun. Like I said, my brother Stephen would have loved this, and his name was written all over it. And I knew that I wasn't him, but I did know that we had long ago discussed how people just don't have fun anymore. They don't know how. He did. And he would have dug what I was doing. I sure was. It was fun. We also would agree with what each of us found to be the keys to our having fun—smiling, singing, laughing, drinkin', women, sex...and music. Definitely music. Because music is fun. But nothing is fun when you start to overthink it or begin reading into it some sort of bullshit, imagined or otherwise.

Day 241-

I went for my round on this morning a little fatigued, a little groggy, but truly aware of what a gorgeous day it was for December. The holiday season was a distant haze. I felt pretty darn good though, in spite of the lack of good sleep. I was, as always, anxious to see the Redhead, come what may never did.

Didn't matter. From the moment I had awaken I'd determined that, yes, I was just putting way too much thought into all this and I didn't want it to stop being fun. It was probably better, I let myself think, to have a little break from it all anyway, so I just walked peacefully back toward home and continued to take in the simple beauty of life, all around me, and enjoy my clearheadedness and peace of mind.

A mind so clear, mind you, that it allowed me the fleeting thought of how "life imitates art," and "music is art," and "art is music," and...shit, here we go again. I then realized that, "Art Lover," by the Kinks, was playing on my iPod as I neared my house. A song about how women, all women, are all works of art, and yes, *I'm an art lover,* I thought, as I slowly pulled my earbuds out and walked through the door.

Day 242-

It was another wonderful December morning as I set out for my round of the parkland. Sleep came to me once I'd decided to let this overthinking stuff go, and to stop making mountains out of molehills, so the dawn found me quite relaxed and happy. I didn't see my gal pal this particular time, but I didn't pay it any mind. I was going to stay happy and the only way to do it would be just playin' like I had all along—not worrying about what other people around, that might hear us, might think about us and the game we were playing with each other. Don't think. Two ships. What's on the box...

Day 243-

Me- BRIDGE OVER TROUBLED WATERS (Simon and Garfunkel)
Her- ANOTHER BRIDGE TO BURN (Waylon Jennings)

Me- HAVE I THE RIGHT? (The Honeycombs)
Her- KNOW YOUR RIGHTS (The Clash)

Me- BEFORE YOU ACCUSE ME (Eric Clapton)
Her- GUILTY (Randy Newman)

Me- HATE ME (Blue October)
Her- ALL I WANNA DO (Sheryl Crow)

Me- WHEN I GET WHERE I'M GOING (Brad Paisley)
Her- C U WHEN U GET THERE (Coolio)

Me- I CAN'T WAIT (John Hiatt)
Her- I CAN WAIT (Steve Earle)

Me- AM I THE ONLY ONE? (The Dixie Chicks)
Her- YOU AND YOUR CRYSTAL METH (The Drive-by Truckers)

Me- SMOKE TWO JOINTS (The Toyes)
Her-DOWN TO SEEDS AND STEMS AGAIN (Commander Cody
    + The Lost Planet Airmen)

Me- SO RIGHT (The Dave Matthews Band)
Her- SO WRONG (Eli Goldsmith)

Me- THE ELEVEN (The Grateful Dead)
Her- THE TWELFTH OF NEVER (Johnny Mathis)

Me- STUPID GIRL (The Rolling Stones)
Her- STUPID BOY (Keith Urban)

Me- STUCK IN A MOMENT YOU CAN'T GET OUT OF (U2)
Her- MY WORST FEAR (Rascal Flatts)

Me- MAMA TOLD ME NOT TO COME (Randy Newman)
Her- MAMA TRIED (Merle Haggard)

Me- I KNOW YOU WON'T (Carrie Underwood)
Her- AS YOU SAID (Cream)

Me- I JUST DON'T KNOW WHAT TO DO WITH MYSELF
    (White Stripes)
Her- GOD ONLY KNOWS (The Beach Boys)

Me- IT DON'T COME EASY (Ringo Starr)
Her- IT HASN'T HAPPENED YET (John Hiatt)

Me- YOU AIN'T GOIN' NOWHERE (The Byrds)
Her- YOU BETTER THIK TWICE (Poco)

Me- IF I COULD BE THERE (Emmylou Harris)
Her- IF I COULD ONLY FLY (Nanci Griffith)

Me- GET NAKED WITH ME (Waylon Jennings)
Her- GET ME OUT OF HERE (Paul McCartney)

Me- IN THIS HOUSE THAT I CALL HOME (The Knitters)
Her- IN THE GHETTO (Elvis Presley)

Me- TOO SICK TO PRAY (Willie Nelson)
Her- THE DOCTOR WILL SEE YOU NOW (Stephen Stills)

Me- GOTTA GIVE IT UP (Marvin Gaye)
Her- GOTTA GET AWAY (The Rolling Stones)

Me- DON'T BE ANGRY (Stonewall Jackson)
Her- DON'T BRING ME DOWN (Eric Burdon + The Animals)

Me- I LOVE YOU BUT I DON'T KNOW WHAT TO SAY (Katey
    Sagal)
Her- DON'T SAY ANYTHING (Madness)

Me- I KNOW YOU RIDER (The Grateful Dead)
Her- I DON'T EVEN KNOW YOUR NAME (Alan Jackson)

Me- I'M DOWN (The Beatles)
Her- I'VE SEEN THAT MOVIE TOO (Elton John)

Me- I JUST WANNA MAKE LOVE TO YOU (Cold Blood)
Her- DO YOU REALLY THINK I CARE? (The Rolling Stones)

Me- DO YOU KNOW WHAT I MEAN? (Lee Michaels)
Her- I JUST CAN'T TAKE IT ANYMORE (Gram Parsons)

Me- EVEN BETTER THAN THE REAL THING (U2)
Her- EVEN WHEN I'M BLUE (Steve Earle)

Me- WE EXIST (Arcade Fire)
Her- IN SPITE OF OURSELVES (John Prine + Iris DeMent)

Me- INFAMY (The Rolling Stones)
Her- FUCK YOU (I'M FAMOUS) (Shooter Jennings + Hierophant)

Day 273-

Two ships, right? Just blowin' their foghorns in the mystic night, right?

Thirty days gone by and I'm not holding back and not falling victim to any subconscious undertones, just shoutin' out what's on the box...

And then all this came down...

Day 274-

Me- WALK A MILE IN MY SHOES (Joe South)
Her- WALKING AROUND SENSE (Patterson Hood) and with the second trip came...
Me- GIVE ME BACK MY HOMETOWN (Eric Church)
Her- FUCK THIS TOWN (Robbie Fulks)

Me- I WANT YOU SO HARD (The Eagles of Death Metal)
Her- YOU SHOULDN'T TAKE IT SO HARD (Keith Richards) along with...
Me- IT'S NOW OR NEVER (Elvis Presley)
Her- FUCK OFF (Kid Rock)

Me- I'M MOVIN' ON (The Rolling Stones)
Her- I'M NOT GONNA MISS YOU (Glen Campbell) and then came...
Me- YOU BETTER LEAVE ME IN THE MORNING (Kristy Dee)
Her- I'M ON MY WAY (The Proclaimers)

Me- FUCK WITH ME (Big Neal)
Her- I WILL (The Beatles) followed up by...
Me- YOU DON'T WANNA FUCK WITH ME (Ol' Dirty Bastard)
Her- I DON'T FUCK WITH YOU (G-Unit)

Me- TRYING TO GET TO HEAVEN (BEFORE THEY CLOSE THE
    DOOR) (Bob Dylan)
Her- YOU BETTER GO NOW (Billie Holiday) with the second
    trip...
Me- I FEEL A SIN COMIN' ON (Pistol Annies)
Her- I CAN'T IMAGINE (Shelby Lynne)

Me- I FOUND A BOY (Adele)
Her- I KISSED A GIRL (Katy Perry)

Me- I CAN RUN WITH THE BIG DOGS (Waylon Jennings)
Her- DOG DAYS ARE OVER (Florence + The Machine)

Me- I HATE MYSELF FOR LOVING YOU (Joan Jett + The
    Blackhearts)
Her- I LOVE IT (Icona Pop)

Me- WHO TOOK THE HAPPINESS OUT? (The Dirty Dozen
    Brass Band)
Her- I THINK I FOUND THE CULPRIT (Jack White)

Me- I'M A LOSER (The Beatles)
Her- I TOLD YOU SO (Keith Urban)

Me- I WAS DRUNK (Alejandro Escovedo)
Her- I UNDERSTAND NOW (Patterson Hood)

Me- I WANNA BE SEDATED (The Ramones)
Her- I'M SO GLAD (Cream) and when she came back around I
    let this fly…
Me- I WANNA FUCK YOU LIKE I'M NEVER GONNA SEE YOU
    AGAIN (Kid Rock)
Her- FUCK YOU (Cee Lo Green)

Day 285-

Well, after those last 12 days I'm now just about 9½ months
into this charade. No smokes. Feeling kinda indifferent about it.
The holidays came and went, and I actually got through them
rather easily, in spite of having a drink or two, here and there.
The marking of the New Year was gone as well, and now my
birthday was due in a day or so. I didn't see the Redhead when
I went out today, and it would turn out that I would not see
her again until many days after that birthday. I couldn't really
remember what the last exchange between us had been, and
even the few before were a slight mental haze.

Day 297-

Maybe it was turning over another year of my life, maybe it
was the number of days that I'd missed seeing Red, but I somehow found myself again looking into the subconscious of it all,
reading between the lines when there probably were none…
what it all meant to me, to her. I even missed my walk this particular morning and that didn't help matters much, as I found
myself wondering if that had even happened at all during these
many days gone by…

Day 298-

Things felt much different today as she came into my line of sight, her doing that awkward jog and me my perp walk.

Me- END OF THE LINE (The Traveling Wilburys)
Her- IT DOESN'T MATTER ANYMORE (Buddy Holly)

Day 299-

Me- A SONG FOR YOU (Leon Russell)
Her- (IT'S) THE SAME OLD SONG (The Four Tops) and then I
    got this coming back...
Me- THIS SONG HAS NO TITLE (Elton John)
Her- THE SONG IS OVER (The Who)

Day 300-

I never saw the girl with the "flamin' red hair" today. Never really saw much of her at all after that. I'd reached a milestone of sorts, but wasn't really so sure of how it all came about, or what had been so easy about it.

I did think about her, a little. Thinking of her was easy, and it was always fun. It didn't last too long, though. I think my mind was just a bit tired, and my feet had mysteriously taken me down the alley by the last turn for home. They led me into the back entrance of my neighborhood liquor store where my aimless fingers dug into the pocket of my walking shorts. I fished out the crumpled twenty-dollar bill that I kept stashed there "just in case."

I bought a pack of Marlboros and snagged a book of matches and slowly walked back home. I plopped my tired old carcass down on my front steps, and just like I'd never missed a beat in 10 months, I fired one up and took a long, somber pull. Well... that was easy.

About This Book-

This is a true story, but the truth ends right about there, where a lot of the stretching of it begins. Everything on these pages happened, just not quite like you are seeing it. I have 10,550 items in my music library, but what I've offered here is just a mere sampling. It is likely obvious that with so much material I could have been a bit more creative, but, admittedly, I'm lazy. What I thought to be a clever notion for a story quickly became corny, then tiresome, and then boring, by the first few pages, I'm sure—

But! You can play your own version of this game! Seriously! Try it, music lovers! Fun!

About Her—

I do still see this young woman from time to time as I still make that same walk nearly every day. We don't really play the "game" anymore as it just kind of faded away (like one of those songs...), and she also has no idea that she is in this novella. It's probably better that way because, for better or worse, and through it all, she remains what I consider to be a good friend.

About Stephen—

He is my brother, and he was bigger than life. Stephen would command your attention and interest, and then win your admiration. What I did when I started this game was all "Stephen." I acted on a whim, doing just what only he would have done, without even realizing it. When I told him about the red-haired girl and all the great items that she had on her iPod, he was so thrilled about it, mostly for me (but I never did tell him that she didn't really have any Waylon Jennings or Grateful Dead). I never did tell him about this little book either, as I never got the chance. Stephen headed off over the Rainbow Bridge much, much too soon. So…this song has no title, but it's for you, Stephen. I love you, and I miss you.

Platitude Of Gratitude—

"Thank you" just may seem a bit worn-out sometimes. Nonetheless, I am extremely grateful for, and would like to thank, these wonderful people—

Red—you're a good sport

Armen, Keith, and Ross—my lead, rhythm, and bass guitars, respectively—
Actually, my trusted proofreaders, editors, and consultants

My wife and daughters—I love you so much—Thank you for putting up with me and all the corny shit I do, and thanks for allowing me to once again pretend that I'm a writer...

9 781478 776819